WHITE FIELD, BLACK SHEEP

WHITE FIELD,

BLACK SHEEP

A Lithuanian-American Life

DAIVA MARKELIS

THE UNIVERSITY *of* CHICAGO PRESS

Chicago & London

DAIVA MARKELIS is associate professor of English at Eastern
Illinois University.

The University of Chicago Press, Chicago 60637
The University of Chicago Press, Ltd., London
© 2010 by The University of Chicago
All rights reserved. Published 2010
Printed in the United States of America
19 18 17 16 15 14 13 12 11 10   1 2 3 4 5

ISBN-13: 978-0-226-50530-5
ISBN-10: 0-226-50530-8

Library of Congress Cataloging-in-Publication Data

Markelis, Daiva.
    White field, black sheep : a Lithuanian-American life / Daiva
Markelis.
        p. cm.
    ISBN-13: 978-226-50530-5 (cloth: alk. paper)
    ISBN-10: 0-226-50530-8 (cloth: alk. paper)
    1. Markelis, Daiva.   2. Lithuanian Americans—Illinois—
Chicago—Biography.   I. Title.
    F548.9.L7M37 2010
    305.891′92073077311—dc22

                                                    2010010263

To the memory of my mother

Contents

The famous lips. Courtesy of Creative Commons/Flickr.

I Was the Child of Teepees

The markers of my childhood: the varnish factory looming like a giant domino against the sooty sky, the rat-infested coal yard north of the Burlington tracks, the pair of huge red Magikist lips jutting out and above the Eisenhower Expressway. Coming back from summer trips to Indiana, my sister and I would spot them and know we were home. They were a woman's lips, curving gracefully at the edges. Set against the gray industrial landscape of northern Cicero, Illinois, they seemed to me heartbreakingly beautiful.

My mother, however, found them vulgar, symbolic of all the things wrong with this new country: plastic flowers, Hostess cupcakes, Barbie dolls. What she found offensive about the Magikist sign was not only the deliberate and ugly bigness of the lips, but also the provocative misspelling of the word. "It should be *magic kissed*, shouldn't it?" she'd say every time we passed the sign. She disliked the loony orthography of

American advertising, hated finding the *s* in *ease* arrogantly displaced by a *z*, as in the over-the-counter sleeping pill, Sleep-Eaze. (In our native Lithuanian there's no mechanism for such an E-Z resettlement of morphemes.)

The Western Electric building on Cicero Avenue, just south of Cermak, formed another boundary marker. Driving home from the Lithuanian Center on Fifty-Seventh and Claremont, my father knew what was coming the moment its Disney-like spire loomed into sight. "Mes jau matom mūsų bokštą," my sister and I would singsong, repeating it over and over until we got home. *Now we see our tower. Now we see our tower.* We lived several blocks away in a two-story brownstone much like all of the other two-story brownstones on the street. Our landlady, Ponia Sereikienė, lived on the floor above us with Stanley, her balding middle-aged son. A huge stuffed eagle guarded the front landing to the apartment, its eyes an unnatural yellow, its wings outspread and claws sharp, ready to pounce on little girls who didn't listen to landladies. You had to get past the ugly bird to get to the treasures in her flat—a risk worth taking, for inside her musty bedroom atop a big brown dresser lay a stack of splendid holy cards, two inches thick, edged with gold, depicting saints with haloes big as Frisbees. St. Therese, the Little Flower of Jesus, and St. Anthony, the patron saint of lost objects. Virgin Marys in all their various guises and several Sacred Heart of Jesuses. She even had the pope—her only pontiff—a hefty man wearing a little white beanie too small for his big head. And, of course, St. Casimir, our only Lithuanian saint—later withdrawn from the panoply, yet another loss in a long and seemingly inevitable string affecting our home country.

It was not only the inordinate beauty of the cards that took my breath away, but also the way they were acquired. At five, I had already been to several wakes—in this large, tight Lithuanian émigré community people were always dying. Mrs. Sereika, however, must have been to hundreds, and this fact alone was enough to give the cards exalted status.

My mother didn't think much of the holy cards. "The Sereikas are different from us," she explained patiently. "Lithuanian, yet not Lithuanian." Ponia Sereikienė added Lithuanian endings to English words. She said "boysas" and "streetas" instead of *berniukas* and *gatvė*. My mother said this was because she had come to America many years ago for economic reasons and had forgotten how to speak the one true Lithuanian language properly: "She's not D.P., like us."

My parents never really explained what a D.P. was. Years later I learned that Displaced Person was the unofficial designation bestowed upon European refugees who had spent time in Ally-governed detention camps in Germany or Austria before being repatriated. Growing up in Cicero, though, I heard only D.P., or, more accurately, T.P.—both my parents pronounced the *D* as a *T*. In first grade we had learned about the Plains Indians, who'd lived in tentlike dwellings made of wood and buffalo skin called *teepees*. In my childish confusion, I thought that perhaps my parents weren't Lithuanian at all, but Cherokee. I went around telling people that I was the child of teepees.

For the most part, our teepee life was an ordinary, somewhat solitary endeavor. My father worked as a draftsman during the day and went to school at night to study engineering, a career he had little interest in and aptitude for. In Dusetos, he had been a teacher of Lithuanian. My mother cooked and sewed and read American decorating magazines and Lithuanian novels. At the University of Vilnius she'd written papers on the East Prussian poet Agnes Miegel, and had planned to write her thesis on Lithuanian elements in Miegel's work when the war broke out and changed everything.

Several times a month my mother suffered from migraines so severe the least bit of light made her nauseous. I remember the orange plastic bucket propped up on a chair next to the bed where she lay moaning, clutching the once-cold washcloth in her hand. On the end table stood a mug of weak, lukewarm tea.

On those days my sister Rita and I would be carted off to our grandparents' apartment across town, a place filled with magical things: a dried polished coconut as big as a little girl's head—the first thing we ran to, petting its smooth dark brown surface—a box of seashells, a flowered tin of postcards from strange places like Florida, a blood-red rose forever preserved in a globe of water. "A crystal ball," Rita would say. We would try to read the future.

Had we been able to read the past, perhaps we'd have seen our grandmother not as a mere old woman who spoke German to the shopkeepers in Cicero, but as a *bajoraitė*, the daughter of aristocratic landowners, sitting at the baby grand piano in the parlor of the manor at Varniai, executing, with a certain luminous precision, the first movement of Beethoven's *Waldstein* Sonata. Her roots extended back to Prussia, the area Eliot alludes to in *The Wasteland: Bin gar keine Russin, stamm' aus Litauen, echt deutsch.* At some point the family migrated eastward, settling in the Lowlands of Lithuania, the region known as Žemaitija. Lowlanders have a reputation for being opinionated and stubborn, idiosyncratic in both speech and action. My sister and I would laugh at the way my grandmother mispronounced the Lithuanian word for *potato*: "It's *bulvė*, not *bulbė*, grandma."

Weekends were sometimes punctuated by visits from my parents' friends, engineers who wanted to be writers, writers who worked for Campbell Soup. I remember the tall frosted glasses, the tang of ginger ale, which my father let me sip—the closest we ever came to pop in our house. That strange word *haiboliukas* (little highball) filtered through the air, the diminutive "*iukas*" added on, I realize today, to disguise the nondiminutive size of the drinks. The women, glamorous with their red lipstick, drank too, though perhaps more slowly, gracefully flicking their cigarettes between sips. The ashes drifted, like dirty snow, into large, oddly shaped ceramic ashtrays.

Perhaps some drank because it's what their fathers did, and their grandfathers before them, finding refuge from the cold Lithuanian nights. The Russian overlords ignored the whiskey—a drunken serf was a manageable serf. Others drank because they were geniuses, their squelched talent too great a burden to bear in this heathen country. That's why Algimantas Mackus drank. His unornamented poems were a disturbance, a violation of proper themes and traditional rhythms. His thin black book of poems about the death of Antanas Škėma, the best modern Lithuanian writer living in exile, was titled *Chapel B*. I was afraid to touch this Lithuanian book with the English name, afraid that if I did, I, too, would soon end up in Chapel B. And then there was Viktoras Petravičius, whose paintings were displayed in a museum in Paris, who now painted on trees and walls and stone.

My mother's explanations about my father's drinking contradict each other, depending on her mood or frame of mind. "Your father never really had a problem. Everyone drank in those days. Certainly everyone in *our* crowd," she'd say. Or, "Oh, I suffered with your father. How I suffered. He'd have too much to drink and then he'd start putting me down, calling me a snob. And then there were those times he'd pass out on the steps and I'd have to drag him in."

Lately I have been talking to my mother about the past, sharing with her these excerpts I jot down and assemble, then reassemble, as if they were pieces of amber forming one of those mosaics of countryside scenes found in Lithuanian living rooms (though not, my mother would be quick to add, *our* living room.) "How do you remember all of this?" she asks. But in truth, my memories of early childhood, of life before English, are few. The therapists with whom I have worked over the years have encouraged me to examine this stage of my life, though only the psychoanalyst pushed for a thorough investigation. He viewed with detached suspicion the claim that mine is a memory geared toward detail, that actual narrative eludes me in therapy as it does in fiction writing. I told him what the novelist Lore Segal had said in a writing workshop I'd attended as an M.A. student—my stories "worked" although nothing much happened in them.

"Life isn't fiction," Dr. G. explained slowly and patiently, as if my problem was not depression, but active psychosis, an inability to distinguish reality from fantasy.

We tried, Dr. G. and I, to uncover those early events that might have had a bearing on my life at twenty-three. I would close my eyes and think really hard, like Dorothy in *The Wizard of Oz* when she wants to go back to Kansas. And then, when I opened my eyes, I would always come up with the same memories, three in all, distinct and crystalline as snowflakes.

In one we are riding, my mother, sister, and I, on the Cicero Avenue bus. We're heading south, perhaps to Alden's to shop for those things not important enough to necessitate a trip downtown. We probably will not buy much. We never do. Not clothes, since she sews those for us herself. Shoes, maybe? How I want that shiny patent leather pair at Florsheim, but they aren't practical, which means they cost too much. My mother is holding my chubby little hand while my sister sits twirling a hank of hair around her finger over and over again, a habit that worries our mother. If we behave well, my mother will reward us with Chunkies. I almost always choose the gold-wrapped one, more for its pretty gilded wrapper than for the almonds inside. An old man steps onto the bus. His hair is gray and matted, matching his clothes. He mumbles to himself as he counts out the change. Worst of all, he smells. No, worst of all, according to my mother, is that he is not wearing any socks. She points this out to us in Lithuanian, and I know from the tone of her voice that she is going to do something embarrassing. When it is time to get off, she takes a dollar bill, our Chunky money, out of her big black purse and slips it, almost imperceptibly, into the old man's hand.

In another it's Christmas Eve. I am three years old, and know enough about Santa Claus, or Kalėdų Senelis, to be practicing the poem *Meškiukas Rudnosiukas*, the Little Bear with the Brown Nose, for weeks. At approximately seven, the doorbell rings. Kalėdų Senelis! My parents seem surprisingly relaxed in his bright red and white presence, as if he were just the milkman stopping by. When he takes a seat on the sofa, however, I notice that under his fluffy white beard, he bears a striking resemblance to Mr. Skruodys, my best friend Daina's father—the same gray bushy eyebrows, the same large brown eyes. I stumble through the poem.

Years later I will ponder the brazenness of Lithuanian Santa Clauses. Not content to merely take their place in a child's imagination by climbing down the chimney, they show up at the door, ring the bell, and invite themselves in.

The last memory is of my grandmother sitting in front of the television, hands folded on her heavy lap. My sister and I are growing tired of this program, heavy men taking turns trying to knock down the funny-looking white plastic bottles with a big black ball. "Močiute," we say, "can we watch cartoons?" But it is two in the afternoon, and there are no cartoons. Grandmother starts explaining the game to us, again, and we tell her that we know, yes, we understand. She just sits there, staring at us. And in that silence I sense there is something wrong, something "off," like lipstick just a shade too orange, like a doily moved an inch and a half from the center of a table.

Writing, pen on paper, slowly and clumsily, like a child climbing a hill, I find memories rising to the edge of consciousness in a way they never seemed to in therapy. Two others have recently broken through the surface, bringing the total number to five.

"This is ridiculous, this numbering of recollections," a friend tells me. "Another manifestation of your obsessive-compulsive disorder."

"Perhaps I'm just bitter," I answer.

Others—white-bread Americans like this friend—have more. They've always had more. When I was growing up they had more toys, more television time, higher allowances. In high school they had better, more expensive clothes. And today, they have more memories, an unbroken line in English. Perhaps all children who make the transition from one language to another lose memories in the passage. Thinking back in English on that part of childhood lived solely in Lithuanian, I feel that I should have amassed a broader repertoire than this.

Memory Number Four.

A cold January morning. The snow promised for Christmas is compensating for its broken pledge by falling in flakes as large as butterflies. Early afternoon finds us out in the yard, my mother in jeans and a parka, my sister and me in snowsuits and woolen mittens. Sculpting the snow into little balls is tougher than it seems—it dissolves in our hands if packed too light, but breaks under the pressure of a firmer touch. The real work, however, comes in pushing the bunched and hardening snow around the yard.

We go inside for the requisite black buttons and carrot. We look for a hat.

"How about this old beret?" my mother asks.

"Snowmen don't wear berets," my sister says with scorn and suggests my father's favorite fedora.

She is about to start crying when my mother remembers the orange pail, the one beside her bed in case a migraine ambushes her. We crown the snowman with a plastic fez. We're thrilled with our Turkish Frosty, but the next morning we rise early to find him decapitated and dismembered, his frozen remains scattered about the yard. We stand at the window, wordless.

Memory Number Five.

I am sitting at the kitchen table with my sister, pasting sheets of Green Stamps into a booklet as our mother supervises from her post at the sink. Watching the pages fill up, the booklet swell, we bask in the intensely pleasurable knowledge that what we are doing isn't just fun and games—we are helping our family. Soon, very soon, next week perhaps, we will walk down to the S&H redemption center on Cermak Avenue where my mother will sift through the catalogue, then decide to get the toaster (or is it the Libby drinking glasses?) against the better judgment of my sister and me, who make a strong case for the ceramic cow-shaped creamer.

Sometimes we must tear the stamped sheets apart and then piece them back together, must complete the inch at the bottom of the page with a single row of stamps. Once, my sister pasted a sheet in upside down. "Look what you've done," I cried. "She's ruined everything, Ma."

How do you remember all of this?

My mother and I are sitting in her condominium in south suburban Oak Lawn. A black-and-white triptych of bare-breasted, big-hipped women dancing with garlands in their hair hangs on the same wall as a large oil of the crucified Christ. I note his face is the shade of a bruised apple.

I am here because my mother is, in her own words, "in bad emotional shape." When this happens I come over and we drink coffee and eat cheesecake. I tell her stories. I count my memories. We discuss the probable causes of her melancholy.

"I walked down to the cemetery yesterday to see your father," she tells me. "They locked me in."

"Who locked you in?"

"The cemetery people. They locked me in. I was there a couple of hours and didn't notice that the sun was setting."

"Ma, why do you need to spend so much time in the cemetery?"

"They must lock the entrance gates at five. I walked over to the main office, but no one was there."

My mother's ongoing dissatisfaction with the management of St. Casimir's Lithuanian Cemetery is mingled with her own sense of guilt at having chosen what she calls the "wrong" section of the cemetery in which to bury my father. The location, she claims, is not central. When I point out that the central locations are all occupied, that all that are left are the peripheries, she replies that, well, then, another periphery, away from the traffic of Pulaski Avenue, would have been better. She talks about moving my father's grave to a more auspicious and accessible part of the cemetery, where the newer, more modern lots are located.

Her concern about my father's grave has to do at least in part with her own anxieties. She is eighty-three years old and sick, though how sick the doctors can't seem to agree on: the news keeps changing.

A few days ago, I took her for an MRI.

"We're looking for the Imagining Center," she stopped a young nurse.

"You mean the *Imaging* Center."

"That's what I said. The Imagining Center."

My sister (*left*) and I, "reading"

White Field

My first day of kindergarten at St. Anthony's School in Cicero, Illinois, I became aware that most of the world spoke a language other than Lithuanian. I knew that English existed, of course. The family that lived next door to us—six or seven blonde athletic children with names like Bobby and Tammy, as exotic and unfamiliar to me as doughnuts— sometimes used this alien speech. Words like *kid* and *snack*, phrases like *shud-up* would drift across the fence into our backyard, where I'd stand at a distance, gazing openmouthed at the barbarians. And there was television—the characters on *Captain Kangaroo* expressed themselves in English. I thought of these as exceptions, however. Now here this tall person, this fluffy-haired *Missus Bokovich*, was announcing that we were to speak English *only*. "No Lithuanian," she repeated, cheerfully but firmly. "*No* Lithuanian." I looked at my best friend Daina. Clearly, this was an unwelcome development in the natural order of things.

Most of my classmates, like myself, had names that future teachers would view as linguistic obstacle courses: Danutė Brusokas and Danutė Vyšniauskas; Arvydas Jašmantas and Audrius Baltaragis and Arūnas Baltrušaitis. There was Raimundas Mičiulis, the school's juvenile-delinquent-in-training, and Saulius Tamošiūnas, who said not one word throughout kindergarten. We had a Ramunas and a Ramunė; an Edmundas and an Edvardas; a Violeta and a Vida. A few of the names had been simplified through several generations of "out of tribe" marriages. Diane Metrick and Wayne Urbik, whose grandfathers had come to this country as Metrikas and Urbikas, spoke only a few words of Lithuanian. Although we vastly outnumbered the half-breeds, we sensed, by the easy way they talked to the teacher, that they were somehow superior. Later they would be exempt from the daily lessons in Lithuanian, the fifty minutes of Lithuanian grammar or history that took place in the afternoons by teachers brought in from the neighborhood.

Except for that first day, I remember almost nothing of kindergarten. Those traditional accoutrements—construction paper and rounded scissors, nap time, even milk and cookies—remain the memories of other children. I vaguely recall coloring in pictures of teapots, but my friend Natalija informs me that we did no such thing.

"We *sang* 'I'm a Little Teapot.' We never colored in teapots."

Perhaps in the process of trying to grasp this new language I forgot everything else.

I don't remember the transition from Lithuanian to English. One day I was listening to a recording of *Skrendantis Paršiukas* (The Little Flying Pig), the next reading from books starring David and Ann, the Catholic Dick and Jane. One day my mother was telling me stories about little bears lost in the woods who find their way home. *Kartą gyveno meškų šeima.* . . . About Little Red Riding Hood. The Lithuanian Red Riding Hood, who didn't get swallowed up by the wolf, but managed to talk her way out of it. The next day I was listening to Sister Sebastian's extended monologues on the goodness of God and the horrors of paradise lost.

I didn't much care for these monologues. I missed my mother's stories, the reassuring cadence of her voice as she read from books printed in Vilnius on cheap-quality paper, stories about mean little girls who abused their dolls and lazy girls who refused to help peel potatoes. How different the books were in school, with this bland David and Ann. There was a pesky younger brother with the absurd name of Little Timmy, and a dog, Skippy, I think, and a cat named Fluffy. David and Ann lived in a big white house, not a two-story brownstone. Not much ever happened to David and Ann—you never even saw David's father walking around with a bottle of beer in his hand.

Reading in English came easily to me. For one thing, I had already been reading in Lithuanian. I had learned from my father, sitting on his lap in the evenings, from a book with pictures illustrating the Lithuanian alphabet. "Lėlė. Repeat again. Lėlė," he would say. "Kėdė. Repeat again. Kėdė." The phonics that Sister Sebastian taught using a book with pictures above the words assured me that the process was similar in English, though with fewer letters, twenty-six compared to thirty-two. There were none of the squiggly lines or *nosinės* dangling from the bottom right of certain letters like mouse droppings, no little hats on the *c*'s or *s*'s. The letter *q* gave me difficulties, though. Why was *queen* spelled the way it was, and not *kween*? And for a long time it was unfathomable that *g* could be hard, as in *good*, or soft, as in *giant*. Lithuanian, with its endless inflections, is more grammatically complex than English, but its pronunciation follows predictable rules—what you see is almost always what you get.

> Black sheep on a white field;
> He who knows them, leads them.

My father, the son of a subsistence farmer and his barely literate wife, used riddles to try to foster critical thinking in his daughters. It didn't always work.

"Are the black sheep raisins?" I asked with hope.

"No."

"If the black sheep are raisins, then the white field would be a piece of toast."

My father smiled.

"Think of the second half of the riddle."

"Are the black sheep stars? Then the white field would be the sky. The sky during the day."

"You're on the right track. Ancient travelers could look at the stars and find their way home."

I was silent.

"The field is a page of a book," he finally said. "And the black sheep are letters. The clever person, the shepherd, is you, the reader."

I pretended to be a shepherd long before I could actually gather the sheep to the fold. I'd hold a favorite book on my lap and *read* the story, so familiar I knew it word for word, stopping every once in a while, like my mother did, to look at my audience, to turn a page. She would nod her head and smile, my sister would look confused, would ask me later to read from a completely different book. "I don't want to read that," I'd say. "That's a silly book."

Our house was filled with books. I remember the different sizes, their arrangements on the shelves. There were Lithuanian books and English books. I could tell them apart, even when I couldn't read. The ones from Lithuania had colorless covers and thin pages that were bound together when the book was new and had to be carefully serrated with a knife. The English books had sturdy backs with glossy, colorful paper jackets.

Years later, I would marvel at the titles, at the rich and promising world they offered. Mika Waltari's *The Egyptian* stood next to Lady Murasaki's *The Tale of Genji*. Cheap John O'Hara paperbacks shared shelf space with *Desire under the Elms*. *101 Tips for Handymen* cohabitated with Norman Vincent Peale's *How to Make Friends and Influence People*. Algimantas Mackus's *Chapel B*, a Lithuanian book with an English title, served as a bridge to the world of Lithuaniana: the poetry of Henrikas Radauskas; Marius Katiliškis's novel with its poetic title, *Miškais Ateina Ruduo (Autumn Comes through the Forests)*; a slim volume mysteriously titled *Alfa ir Omega*.

As a young child, however, I would sit cross-legged on the floor and leaf through the books in hopelessness and confusion, trying to unlock the code to the secrets of my parents' universe. What was on these pages that gave them such pleasure? Sometimes I looked at the books with fear. My mother had told me about a few of the writers, friends of hers who had died during the war. I began to see their words as tiny little gravestones in an endless white cemetery. Sometimes paging through the older volumes I'd come upon pressed flowers: an iris, its blue petals translucent with age, or a once-blooming rose, now dry and flattened, dead, like the letters on the page.

For years, like the English and Lithuanian books that coexisted peacefully on the living-room shelves, I was bilingual, equally fluent in both languages according to the traditional definition of the term. In school, of course, we spoke English, sometimes reluctantly, evidence of another language present in our rolling *r*'s, our overly aspirated *p*'s. We struggled with idioms and prepositional phrases: for mistake Columbus found America, the party will be in Nata's house. But the accents faded with each passing year, and words that had seemed cumbersome became as familiar as the breakfast cereals we begged our parents to buy.

Television reinforced the English we spoke at school. My parents limited viewing to an hour a week, with an additional hour on weekends. For many years the weekly show was the inculpable *Daktari*, chosen not by my sister and me, who would have much preferred *The Monkees* and *The Brady Bunch*, but by my father, who frequently utilized his veto power in the realm of television programming. He enjoyed watching the competent blonde Paula fighting poachers and poisonous snakes, assisted on occasion by Clarence the Cross-eyed Lion and Judy the Chimp.

There were exceptions to the one-hour rule. The most notable was the Miss America Pageant. I loved the Miss America Pageant, its combination of high drama and routine predictability. My sister and I cheered for the girls with the biggest hair and the flashiest evening dresses. My father was partial to the blondes, of whom there were many. My mother's criteria were the strictest: a long neck, high cheekbones, a "womanly" figure (no bony shoulders or chicken legs), a graceful walk. She viewed the taller candidates with approval. "There are many tall women in the pageant," she would point out. My mother was 5'9". Her most astute critical commentary was saved for the talent competition. The young women who played the piano gained her immediate admiration, unless they chose something outside of the classical repertoire—"Theme from Love Story," for example—in which case they'd be dismissed as rank beginners, worse than if they had performed on the banjo. My mother's unwavering contempt was saved for the baton twirlers, whom she deemed both vulgar and ridiculous: "Where is the talent involved in waving around a long thick stick?"

In addition to the pleasure of placing bets on our favorites, watching the pageant offered us insights into mainstream American culture. We were made more keenly aware not only of the type of beauty that was admired in this country, but also of the values and behaviors it held dear: an outspoken patriotism, bereft of nuance; an enthusiastic but not overly passionate profession of faith in God; a cheery perseverance in the face of obvious defeat.

I grew up wanting to be Miss Illinois, an ambition my mother encouraged, as she encouraged all of my ambitions: altar girl, astronaut, broadcast journalist. I already had a head start: I was tall and fair-haired. I'd have to change my name, though, to something more pronounceable—Debbie Mark, perhaps.

"You already know how to play the piano," my mother said.

More effective in improving our English than *Daktari* and the Miss America Pageant were the commercials, especially the snappy jingles, which my sister and I memorized in order to impress our non-Lithuanian-speaking friends: *It's not how long you make it, it's how you make it long. You wonder where the yellow went when you brush your teeth with Pepsodent.* The Anglos were always one step ahead of us, trumping our pathetic attempts at hipness by casually tossing out words and phrases whose tantalizing meanings eluded us: *out in left field, old man, sloshed.*

English-speaking adults also had access to this mysterious dictionary. When Diane Stakulis's mother invited me out to dinner with her family, a momentous occasion—restaurant meals were as rare as hearty laughter from the nuns—she tried to dampen my elation with "The place is nothing, really, just a greasy spoon."

In my nine-year-old mind, the term sounded wonderful—a shiny silver object of a place.

"A greasy spoon! A greasy spoon! I'm going to a greasy spoon," I gushed to my mother.

At home, my parents talked to my sister and me in Lithuanian. They watched for the intrusion of English words into our speech the way high school biology students look under a microscope for germs.

My parents spoke Lithuanian to us in the streets, on buses, in stores.

"Your children don't seem to be speaking English," a neighborhood woman once reproached my mother.

"They speak English at school," my mother answered.

"You know what they say. 'You can't have your cake and eat it, too.'"

Having borne the collective guilt of leaving their homeland in the hands of the enemy, my parents' generation was not about to shoulder the responsibility for the death of the oldest living European language (as we were told it was again and again).

And there was the chance, infinitesimal as it was, that the Russians would leave Lithuania, evicted by the superior force of the United States, whose leaders, realizing that their blind acceptance of the Molotov-Ribbentrop Pact had been a mistake of the most horrible kind, would go to any length to rectify their error. And then we could go back—we could all go back.

Of course, we did not go back.

We never grilled hamburgers on the Fourth of July, or watched parades. February 16—that was our independence day. Lithuanian Independence Day. We would gather in the crumbling auditorium of St. Anthony's School to celebrate the independence of a nonexistent country. Someone would read a speech about freedom and someone else would read a poem about a country with blue skies and fearless heroes. For many years I was that someone, the reader of poems. The *tautiniai rūbai* I wore, literally translated as *national clothing*—the heavy linen skirt reaching to the floor, the blouse with billowing sleeves, a vest lined in satin with heavy bronze clasps, an embroidered apron, a sash, a string or two of cumbersome amber beads—added twenty pounds to my already chubby frame.

As much as I hated my Lithuanian costume, I took my responsibility as the reader of poems seriously. In everyday life I was a quiet little girl, afraid of strangers, wary of crowds. When I read poetry, however, I loved the attention I received from little old ladies who beamed with approval and from Saturday School teachers ever watchful for mistakes in pronunciation and even from my classmates who eyed me narrowly and who—I was convinced—were consumed with envy. I'd be nervous at first, but then I'd take a deep breath and pretend I was a genie living in a bottle, allowing words to escape, slowly, one by one, like little puffs of smoke:

> Beloved country,
> you have seen
> many
> sorrows.

Sometimes it was my duty to pin the white carnation on a visiting dignitary, usually a politician who appeared around election time extolling the virtues of the hardworking Lithuanians in his precinct or district. Most of the time these visitors were men with greasy pants and shady reputations. Years later I would see their pictures on the cover of the *Cicero Life*. There were legitimate politicians as well, such as Judy Barr Topinka, the state representative of our district, who many years later was elected the state treasurer of Illinois. She was of Czech descent, and sympathized with our cause. And there was Henry Hyde, the conservative congressman from neighboring Oak Park. There's a photograph of me in my *tautiniai rūbai* with Hyde. A silk handkerchief peeps out of the pocket of his navy-blue suit; the white carnation is already drooping. With his heavy white pomaded hair, his girth, he looks like a slightly lascivious Captain Kangaroo.

There came a day—too soon, my mother would have said—when English surpassed its rival in the struggle for linguistic supremacy. English seemed direct and simple, flexible as a Slinky. The misspellings that my mother derided—*cheez* for *cheese*—were just further indications of the general superiority of English over Lithuanian—its simplicity, its boldness, its sense of play. Lithuanian sentences seemed to go on and on, twisting and turning, like a forest path that eventually led you back to the very spot from which you started. Speaking Lithuanian meant being corrected, again and again, by parents or Saturday School teachers or well-meaning neighbors.

"What's on television?" I would ask in Lithuanian.

"The antenna is on the television," my father would answer.

Once I had to write a condolence note in Lithuanian and asked my father to proofread it.

"Atsiprašau. . . . ," I began.

"Atsiprašau?" my father said, his thick eyebrows raised in disbelief.

"*Atsiprašau* means *I'm sorry.* As in 'I'm sorry to hear about the death of your mother,'" I answered, annoyed at my father's ignorance.

"You can't say *atsiprašau.* It sounds as if you were somehow responsible for the death."

"So what do I say?" I asked in exasperation.

"You have to say *užuojauta.*"

For years I dreaded Lithuanian wakes, fearing that instead of saying *užuojauta* I would say *atsiprašau.* I prayed that no one in our community would die, or that they would wait until I grew up and moved out of the house.

....

In the past few months I have gotten practice saying *užuojauta.* My mother's friends keep dying with alarming regularity. She attends all of their wakes and funerals, asking me to drive her to the Petkus Funeral Home and then, if she can't find a ride, to St. Casimir's Cemetery. She doesn't seem particularly distressed by these deaths, and neither do her remaining friends. After the requisite silent prayer at the foot of the body, the necessary *užuojautas,* they sit around the funeral home as if they were remaining contestants on some macabre reality show, sad for their friends who have had to leave the island, but happy to have evaded elimination for yet another round.

The idea that I will one day lose my mother, that the day is closer than either of us will care to admit, fills me with an utter sadness. I took her to the doctor yesterday. The news is bad: There is a lump where her left ovary used to be.

"The size of a baseball," said the doctor.

"How big is a baseball?"

"Okay, the size of an orange."

"A big orange or a small orange? Or is it more like a tangerine?"

I try to envision a life without her, without the delicate intimacy we have built up over the years, one sometimes strained by silly arguments, more often strengthened by my mother's stories and jokes, by her unbridled confidence in whatever I choose to undertake. I talk to her daily on the phone, try to visit her once a week, making the drive up on weekends from Berwyn, where I live with the man I will marry in a few months. Sometimes he joins me and listens to my mother's stories of life in the Old Country. My mother likes Marty, whom she sometimes calls Martynas, perhaps in an effort to fool herself that he is Lithuanian. Other times she pronounces his name in what she believes is the phonetically correct version—Mort-ee. "Is Mort-ee coming with you?" she will ask. Or, "How is Mort-ee doing?"

Driving north on Pulaski after visiting my mother, I pass the large wooden Indian standing atop a vision center like Christ the Redeemer in Rio de Janeiro. I used to think this Indian protected the surrounding streets of Chicago's South Side with its resident Poles and Lithuanians and Irish and Mexicans. The Indian holds one hand up in a brave salute. He has been here forever.

"How," my sister would say when we passed him.

"How," I would answer.

My mother, of course, found the Indian extremely vulgar.

On Cicero Avenue I pass the Western Electric Tower, *my tower, our tower*. The surrounding buildings, which once made up the Hawthorne

Works complex, have been torn down. In their place now stands a strip mall with an Omni Superstore and a Jennifer Sofabeds. A little further north the Acapulco School educates a new generation of drivers. The old laundromat is now a *lave rápido*. Everybody speaks Spanish here.

My old grammar school is still where it used to be, red brick with white trimming, the words *Švento Antano Mokykla* engraved in stone, though the last Lithuanian student graduated years ago. A narrow courtyard separates the school from the convent. The church, built in 1906, and its adjacent rectory complete what used to be a self-contained little world. A wrought-iron fence links them all—school, rectory, church, and convent.

I imagine the children in kindergarten. Does the teacher tell them, "No Spanish," in a firm yet cheerful voice? Do they look at one another in bewilderment? Do they perceive her words as a challenge, a question, an unwelcome development in the natural order of things?

Šv. Antano Parapijos Mokykla, Cicero, Illinois

The Sin also Known as Disappear

"You are capable of sin," Sister Gemma announced one gloomy February morning.

"Do you know what this means?" she asked, slowly surveying the room.

We nodded solemnly.

We had no idea what she was talking about.

"It means you are adults."

We were in third grade, preparing to make our First Communion.

Sister discussed the three categories of sin as if she were trying to sell us automobiles: "We have your venial, your mortal, and, of course, your very first, your original." *Original* we didn't have to worry about. We weren't responsible for that fatal lack of judgment in the Garden of Eden that had started the ball of damnation rolling. *Venial* sins seemed to be our lot as third graders. As practice for the First Confession, we brainstormed age-appropriate venials—coveting a playmate's toy, talking back to parents.

"You're not above committing mortal sins, so you shouldn't get too cocky," Sister warned. *Cocky* was one of her favorite words, along with *hooligan, pantywaist,* and *horseplay.*

The class fell silent.

"Murder and missing Mass are two examples of mortal sins," she explained, as if we were as likely to commit one as the other.

"All sins, however, can be forgiven," she said. Then, as if she had forgotten an item on a grocery list, she added: "Except for one."

"Burying someone alive?" Jonas Žibutis had the nerve to ask.

Sister shook her head.

I raised my hand timidly. My mother had told me about all of the people murdered because they were Jewish, like her classmate Dina in Klaipėda, and all of the people killed because they held property, or were teachers, like my Uncle Justinas; he had been shipped off to a place so cold people froze to death like statues in Freeze Tag.

"Does it start with the letter *gee*?" I asked.

"It starts with an *ess*," Sister hissed.

"Is it the sin committed by a man named Stalin?" I continued. "Or by a man named Hitler?"

"Committed by Judas," Sister barked. "Not when he betrayed our Lord, but the next day when he slipped into the abyss of eternal darkness."

We must have looked confused.

"Suicide. The sin also known as *despair*," she explained.

The word I heard was *disappear.* The word I slowly printed out in my Big Chief notebook was *disappear.*

"It's *despair*, not *disappear*, stupid," said Arvydas Žygas, looking over my shoulder. Then, in an unbearably loud voice, he asked: "Hey, how do you like dis pair of shoes I have?"

Jonas Žibutis guffawed. Arvydas chuckled at his own joke, as he always did. Laughter spread across the room like smoke. Soon everyone was laughing except for me and Sister Gemma and a moonfaced girl who was new at school and whose parents, it was rumored, were divorced.

My mother took little stock in the stories and proclamations of the nuns, in Catholicism in general. No framed pictures of the Sacred Heart of Jesus graced our walls, no *Our Daily Visitor* made its way onto our doorstep. My mother's parents had both been agnostics, prominent social democrats in Lithuania who believed that the road to salvation lay in education, not religion. And although my mother drifted toward a vague and liberal Christianity as she got older, she remained disdainful of evangelism of any kind. Once, when the Jews for Jesus were out in full force in downtown Chicago with their long hair and their cheaply printed pamphlets depicting Jesus as a young Rodney Dangerfield, she stopped a young proselytizer.

"Does your mother know about this?" she asked. "You should be ashamed of yourself. A nice Jewish boy like you."

The day that I learned about despair, I came home and quizzed my mother.

"What's the only sin that can't be forgiven?" I asked her, acting like a little game show host.

"As long as we all love each other, God doesn't mind what we do."

"Ma, that's not what the nun said."

I told her about Judas jumping into the abyss of eternal darkness.

She had the same look she wore the day Sister Salvatore told us about the boy who drowned in Lake Michigan. He had skipped Sunday Mass to go fishing. I had come home to tell my mother she had better start going to church, or, at the very least, never go near a fishing rod. I was now afraid she would march over to the rectory and lecture the nun, who would nod her head politely but make me stay after school for a week to practice writing my capital *O*'s.

Instead, my mother's face softened, and she gently took my hand.

"God forgave Judas. If you want to know what I think."

I wondered briefly if my mother had some secret, privileged connection to the Almighty. For someone who rarely went to church, she interpreted Catholic doctrine as freely as the pope.

The nuns at St. Anthony were the Sisters of St. Casimir, a Lithuanian order founded in Scranton, Pennsylvania, in 1907. They were the daughters of the earlier wave of Lithuanian immigrants, coal miners and meatpackers and steel workers. Their parents had instilled in them not only the tenets of a rigorous Catholicism, but also a loyalty to Lithuania, one only slightly tarnished throughout the years, alloyed as it was with the base metal of American culture—baseball, Boys Town, bake sales. For decades they had taught children who could have been their younger siblings, boys and girls from working-class backgrounds destined to working-class futures, students whose parents worked at Western Electric or Brach's Candy, or owned taverns or corner groceries, whose Lithuanian was an amalgam of English words and Lithuanian suffixes.

With the influx of Lithuanian refugees after the war, however, the sisters were faced with an entirely different set of customers. We, the children of the Displaced Persons, entered kindergarten speaking no English at all, though we knew who Mozart was and could count to fifty and recite entire verses of *Meškiukas Rudnosiukas*. Many of our parents had not only finished high school in Lithuania, but had attended college as well. Many were teachers themselves, others, doctors and engineers. In the eyes of the sisters, however, we were no more special than the sons and daughters of previous generations of Lithuanian immigrants. What mattered was that we be raised to be good Catholics, educated to respect the authority of the Church and, it followed, the Sisters of St. Casimir.

The nuns took their responsibilities seriously, doing their best to answer in an afternoon metaphysical questions that had confounded centuries of Catholic theologians. In the course of an ordinary school day, numbingly simple lessons were juxtaposed with mind-bogglingly complex ideas. One minute we'd be reading "Young Citizens of Timber Town," the next discussing the existence of evil and the purpose of suffering. Classroom spelling bees were followed by discourse into God's omniscient nature.

Religion seeped into every subject. Because we had so thoroughly internalized Catholic tenets of faith, it was difficult to see the universe as anything other than the stage for the unfolding drama between God and Satan; the laws of the universe were constant and immutable because they were put into place by a Maker sure of His purpose. Science seemed unnecessary and dull. Who cared about the distance between the sun and the moon? We were more interested in why there were so many stars. How had God decided on a number? How did God know when to stop?

"Why *did* God create the universe?" we asked.

The answers varied depending on the teacher we had that year: God was lonely, or God was bored, or we won't know until Final Judgment Day, or don't ask such questions.

Religion penetrated geography and history the way a torrid rain saturates a dry and arid plain. The Rocky Mountains, the Grand Canyon, the Sahara Desert, the Nile River, the Arctic Circle—all were examples of God's magnanimity in creating so vast and interesting a universe. The signing of the Magna Carta, Columbus's discovery of America, the abolition of slavery—all were evidence of the manifestation of God's will through the deeds of good Christian men. In fourth grade I wrote a poem, "The First Thanksgiving," that reveals the extent to which I had bought into this melding of religious sentiment and historical reality:

> Everyone tried to shoot a turkey,
> They wanted to get a hundred at least,
> For there, would be a lot of people
> thanking God,
> At the first Thanksgiving feast.
>
> They thanked God and so should we,
> For our food clothes and our family.
> To God we should always pray
> Not just on Thanksgiving day!

Dreadful illustrations—roast turkeys that look as if they might float right off the page, Indians twice the size of Pilgrims—accompany a text rife with dubious historical details.

By the time I was nine, the saints in heaven seemed more real than the Tyrolean yodelers in lederhosen and feathered caps that appeared in our geography textbook, the angels more appealing than David and Ann in *This Is Our Parish*. My parents began to worry. They raised their eyebrows in unison when I told them that the quickest way to sainthood was through martyrdom.

"Is that so?" my mother questioned.

"Yes. And when I grow up I want to be a martyr."

"Like your mother," said my dad and chuckled.

Saints and martyrs need their accoutrements, but my request for yet another leather-bound prayer book, this one in baby blue, was quickly nixed. We had no money for a rosary made of authentic faux pearls. And a black lace mantilla to cover my head at mass was out of the question.

"Ask the good sister to tell you about Vatican II," my father instructed me.

I loved our church. I loved the statue of St. Anthony holding the Christ Child as confidently as a loaf of bread, the Virgin Mary with her pale cheeks tinged with rose eyeing heaven. I loved the incense at early morning Mass, so heavy it stuck to my clothes. I even loved the funeral masses; my favorite part was when the black-robed priest circled the coffin twice, sprinkling holy water, reciting the prayer of the dead in Latin: *Requiem aeternam done ei, Domine.* At home I donned my father's favorite black sweater. Filling an empty salt shaker with water, I performed the funeral rites on my unsuspecting sister's teddy bears.

I found comfort from my childish fears in prayer, discovered in the solace of ritual an antidote to the frequent chaos at home. My mother's migraines, which left her bedridden and morose, were often followed by bursts of manic creative activity where she'd invite my friends over for hours of finger painting or dancing to Tchaikovsky or elementary

German lessons. My father's behavior during my early school years encompassed teary drunken smiles and baffling withdrawal and sudden rages over missing black sweaters. And in a house where the gloom of the Second World War managed to cast a shadow over even the sweetest moments, where my parents would often remind us that life was difficult and unfair, and that others—Americans—who thought differently were naive fools, imagining heaven gave me a deep sense of consolation.

Today I hold on to the remnants of my earlier faith. I suspect that atheist friends mock my clumsy search for grace. They don't know how often my thoughts loop around themselves, keeping me up at night with their bleak rhythm—*cause, effect, cause, effect*—before they flower into mystery.

I can't please the other side either. "You read Walker Percy, but not the Bible," a friend complains. One woman, the daughter of a famous preacher, goes on about the goodness of God. "He wants the best for us," she says. Tell that to my grandmother, I want to say, whose brother disappeared into the vast Stalinist night along with his Jewish wife, whose nephew was slaughtered in the woods of Marijampolė, a martyr for the cause of Lithuanian autonomy.

I tell her about the suicide of a great-great aunt in the 1890s. She walked into a lake in Suvalkija with rocks in her pockets. She was old but in good health, a wise and respected farmer's wife, a loving mother. No one talked about her death in the fleeting decades of the first independence or during the period after the Second World War—suicide was almost as much a scandal during the forty-five-year Soviet occupation as it was during the previous era of freedom.

"She's still burning in hell, I suppose," I tell my friend.

"Protestants don't consider suicide an unforgivable sin."

"They don't?"

"Catholics believe that only a priest can absolve one's sins. In confession," she says in the same tone of voice I used with my mother as a little girl.

I am back in third grade with my anxious classmates. *Bless me father, for I have sinned. This is my first confession.* We've rehearsed these lines in class, gone over them again and again. We strain to hear the private disclosures of our classmates, then whisper our own.

"Speak up," the old priest says. "I can't understand a word you're saying."

And then Sunday morning, in starched white dresses we'll wear only once and tiny pearl tiaras, we march nervously down the aisle at church, little brides of Christ, shortest girls in front. Behind us the boys, fidgety in navy blue suits. Earlier in the morning we were consumed by anxiety, weakened by the obligatory fast, in our minds the story of the boy who, just hours before he was to make his First Communion, foolishly, absentmindedly, chewed a piece of gum. *What was he thinking?* And now, the bigger worry, the wafer—God's body—in our mouths. *Don't chew, now, just let it dissolve.* What if we drop it? What if it—God—falls out of our mouths and onto the ground, stuck to the gray marble floor of St. Anthony's? We walk back to our pews slowly, tight-lipped, pursemouthed.

Afterward—relief. Breakfast in the parish hall. And gifts of rosaries and cash.

° ° ° ° ° ° ° ° ° ° ° ° °

My mother and I are at Wig World, a small room filled with plastic heads, mostly white with red lipstick, covered with wigs from the Eva Gabor collection. Most are curly, with too much hair, making the faces on the plastic heads look tiny.

My mother takes her time trying on wigs: short, long, feathered, curled, dark brown, chestnut, ash-blond.

"How'd I look like as a redhead?"

"I don't think so, mom."

"I want something natural. All of these look fake!" she tells the saleslady, who was all smiles when we entered the store, going on about how Wig World loves its cancer patients, but is now growing tired of the time and attention my mother is demanding.

"You have to style them, you know."

Her final choice is a short glossy auburn with subtle blond highlights.

We leave the store having shelled out over two hundred dollars, including thirty for the necessary special wig shampoo and conditioner.

"Wait, I almost forgot your gift," the saleslady says. "It's an angel pin. To keep you safe."

Once outside, my mother examines the pin.

"I'm supposed to wear this cheap thing? It couldn't have cost more than a dollar."

As I pull out of the parking space, a car from the left lane swerves into ours, missing us by a quarter of an inch.

"See," my mother says, "it doesn't even work. We almost got killed."

My friend Daina (*right*) and I

During the Reign of Vytautas the Great

Every Saturday morning, for seven years of my life, while other children were watching cartoons, I studied Lithuanian history and geography, literature and grammar, in the classrooms of St. Anthony's School. They seemed different on this day, these rooms, transformed from the orderly pristine spaces of the nuns, where during the week we sat, hands crossed, the girls in our prim green-and-white uniforms, the boys in navy pants and white shirts, to brighter, more chaotic, chambers where little learning appeared to take place.

We didn't know enough, my sister and I, to protest this infringement of inalienable childhood pleasures—imagine, no Bugs Bunny. By the time we realized that most children did not have to wake up early Saturday morning and march off to school once again, it was too late. Not that out protests would have made a difference. We were told, again and again, how lucky we were to be able to attend a second school. We were "richer" than those poor *amerikonai* who spoke only one language, and mundane English at that.

At the beginning of each semester of Lithuanian Saturday School, we received notebooks in bright orange and lime green and mustard yellow with portraits of Maironis, Father of Lithuanian Poetry, and Vincas Kudirka, Freedom Fighter, on each cover—one notebook per subject. We drew fancy mustaches on Maironis, and otherwise defaced the notebooks. We made fun of the teachers, who had received their pedagogical training in Lithuania. We laughed at their fractured English, hurled spitballs at them, mangled their drawn-out Lithuanian names.

Among our victims was Ponia Motušienė, a short woman with perfect posture, which just accentuated her massive bosom, a chest so huge we wondered how it was able to stay in an upright position. "What about the laws of gravity?" we snickered every time she entered the room. Her colleague, Ponia Klioriené, had inky black hair she wore in a huge bee's nest updo. We dropped the "ienė" ending from her name, substituting "ox," not because she was large or clumsy, but because the resulting Kliorox—Clorox!—was too tempting to resist. "Have you done the reading for Clorox's class?" we'd ask each other.

Some of us had Ponia Babrauskienė, who pronounced her *l*'s like *w*'s. Her speech impediment came most clearly into play the day the class was to read aloud Balys Sruoga's famous poem, *Supasi, supasi lapai nubudinti* (The Awakened Leaves Are Swaying, Swaying).

"Supasi, supasi *w*apai nubudinti," began Arvydas Žygas.

"It's not wapai," Babrauskienė corrected him. "It's wapai!"

"That's what I said. Supasi, supasi wapai nubudinti."

And then there was poor Ponas Zailskas, a good man, old-fashioned, courtly, but too proud and stubborn to wear the hearing aid he so desperately needed. We mouthed out answers to his questions about the dative case, shaping words with our lips. "Speak up," he'd say. We'd whisper back, "But we are speaking up," contorting our faces into manic imitations of speech.

And yet we learned. We conjugated verbs: *Aš matau, tu matai, jis / ji mato* (I see, you see, he / she sees). We wrote *diktantai* (dictation) on the board, fearing a sentence with too many *nosinės*, those squiggles appended to certain vowels to indicate nasality, literally translated as "handkerchiefs." We discussed with great seriousness the uses of the personal pronoun *tu* versus the formal *jūs*. We memorized poems, which we then had to recite on various public occasions—Lithuanian Independence Day, Mother's Day, the end of the school year. They were adult poems about death and heroism and the loss of freedom, about nature and God.

At Lithuanian Saturday School I learned a geography imbued with longing—Lithuania was a country of lush pine forests and golden dunes, a paradise on earth, forever embedded in amber. More important, I learned about the arbitrariness of borders, that a country can exist for one person and not for another—a lesson reinforced at home, where there were always maps, and a globe that my sister and I loved to twirl when my father wasn't around.

Depending on the politics of the mapmaker, Lithuania was either on the map, its borders penciled in with dashes, lines less certain than those that outlined France or Turkey, with the word *Lithuania* squeezed in (or sometimes, oh so wonderfully, *Lietuva*, the Lithuanian spelling), or it was missing, absent, obliterated by a large pink smear of color—the U.S.S.R.

At Lithuanian Saturday School I learned that words can be borders, imposed artificially, that "the Baltic States" were not a complete, unbreakable little set of countries—Lithuania, Latvia, Estonia—but a term conceived during the nineteenth century out of political expediency. Throughout the ages, Lithuania's history has been more firmly, closely linked with Catholic Poland's than with Lutheran Latvia's, although Lithuania's language, like Latvia's, is Baltic, not Slavic.

Lithuanian history, as taught by Juozas Kreivėnas, was my favorite subject. I learned (and still remember), that the Battle of Žalgiris (Tannenberg) was fought in 1410; the Lithuanian army mortally wounded the Teutonic Knights. And I learned that the Treaty of Lublin, signed in 1569, which united Lithuania and Poland, made it impossible for a Lithuanian ever again to ascend the throne, though it allowed for the expansion of these two countries from the Baltic to the Black Sea. And most important, I learned that on February 16, 1918, Lithuania declared its independence from Russia and was able to act on this declaration to become a free nation for the first time in centuries, an independence that lasted until the Communist takeover in 1940 (and would not be regained for another fifty-one years.)

Kreivėnas was a heavy man whose gray suits were worn too thin for respectability and who, according to American standards, could have showered more frequently. We rarely made fun of him, though. We respected him; perhaps we even feared him a little. He made us believe that nothing was more important than what had transpired in the forests of Žalgiris more than five hundred years ago. Unless it was the conversion of the Lithuanian pagans, the last Europeans to accept Christianity, in the middle of the thirteenth century. Nothing was more interesting than the brave and wily Vytautas's attempts to be crowned king of Lithuania, nothing more tragic than the interception of the crown by the Poles on its way to Rome just days before his death.

"During the reign of Vytautas the Great," Kreivėnas would begin; we sat, entranced.

Long after I had graduated from Saturday School, I would visit Kreivėnas in his bungalow filled with books. He owned more books that anyone I knew. He kept them stacked in piles up to the ceiling, until the house could no longer contain them, then transformed his garage into a bookstore, where you could borrow and browse and even buy, for quarters, books printed in Vilnius on cheap paper, poorly bound.

There were people in our community who were suspicious of these books, suspicious of Kreivėnas himself. How to explain all that literature from Communist Lithuania when any correspondence was difficult; the latest dictionaries; the boring novels of proletarian life; the volumes of poetry that attempted and sometimes managed to circumvent the ruling order by playing with language—flattening words out so that they no longer meant what one thought they meant.

The attacks on Kreivėnas were a manifestation of a larger rift, one that threatened to tear apart the once sturdy cloth of the Lithuanian immigrant community, not just in Cicero, Illinois, but in Cleveland and Brockton and Brooklyn and Detroit. Opposing political ideologies had been a part of Lithuanian life since the nineteenth century, but they had been buried in the postwar years when more pressing concerns—finding a job, a place to live, a school to educate one's children—supplanted earlier divisions. More important, everyone was united in their hatred of the Soviets.

Then, sometime in the seventies, the thawing of the cold war was met not with a unified sigh of relief, but a resurgence of the old quarrels. When the Lithuanian government opened its doors to the children of the immigrants in the form of month-long summer courses on the Lithuanian language, the arguments centered on whether one could visit Communist Lithuania and not become a Communist oneself. Those who believed in fostering connections to the occupied homeland were perceived as traitors by those who held to a "We won't go back until every Communist is dead" philosophy.

My parents belonged to the former group. My father, as head of the Cicero chapter of the Lithuanian Society, had spoken out about the need to support the young people who had chosen to travel to Lithuania.

"What the heck, I might even go with them," he said at a meeting to scattered applause and ominous murmurs.

On a bright Saturday morning in the middle of May sometime in the seventies, my mother ran up the two flights of stairs holding a pair of pruning shears like a weapon. She lunged into the kitchen where my father was finishing breakfast and my sister and I were arguing about whose turn it was to clean the bathroom: "Come look! Look what they've done!"

We scurried downstairs.

Giant slashes of bloody red paint covered our garage door; sections of the original brown peeked through, making our garage look like a giant Rauschenberg canvas.

We stared at our garage, my mother shaking, my father frowning. I felt a surge of illicit excitement. My parents, who complained about taxes, who subscribed to *Consumer Reports*, who had voted Republican in the last local election, were Communists!

Several weeks later my father came back from work to find a note written in Lithuanian attached to the doorknob of the front entrance to the house. He read it out loud to us before dinner:

"All you know how to do is hate and destroy, hate and destroy. Stop your hating and destroying before you tear apart the community, you slimy toad of a Communist."

There was no signature to the letter.

"It sure is poorly written," said my father, who had been a teacher of Lithuanian back in Aukštaitija: "Look, no comma after *griauti!*"

My mother was frightened, ready to call the police. My father looked at her and laughed. "No comma after *griauti*," he repeated several times, shaking his head. "No comma after *griauti*."

My mother as a young woman

Mongrel Tongue

My mother's English was always better than my father's. It was a point of pride. My father earned more money at the engineering firm where both worked, he as an engineer, she as a draftswoman. His sense of direction was keener. He may have even spoken Lithuanian with more precision and finesse (though this was a matter of ongoing debate), coming as he did from the Aukštaitija region of the country. But she, my mother, spoke the better English.

My father conceded this point, somewhat reluctantly, arguing that my mother was more fluent because she talked more. She was always talking, talking, talking, blurting out whatever was on her mind. Like most Lithuanian women.

"I'm just naturally gifted when it comes to languages," my mother would answer.

And who could argue? Her German was even better than her English, her French *passable*, her Russian enough to allow her to read the simpler poems of Pushkin.

What she failed to mention in these conversations, however, were her early advantages, the good schools and the expensive books and the maid that had freed my mother from household chores. Her father had been the principal of a prestigious private high school in Kaunas. The artifacts of my mother's life attest to privilege: an emerald necklace lost while playing in the woods of Marijampolė when she was nine; shoes the color of cherries bought on a trip to Stockholm; Agatha Christie paperbacks read at night with the flashlight beneath her blanket, on constant watch for my grandmother, who believed that a good night's sleep was vital for mental health and the proper regulation of the menses.

My father's parents were subsistence farmers, living from day to day on potatoes, apples, and mushrooms, harvesting wheat when the summers obliged. Politically the family leaned to the left—my father's father read the *Social Democrat* and frequently praised the revolution, walking around the little house singing the *Marseillaise* in broken, perverted French. The neighboring farmers called him a Bolshevik, though my father suspects that this had less to do with political beliefs than with the fact that his father rarely went to church and often appeared at the dinner table having forgotten to remove his cap—both clear signifiers of advanced and irreparable bolshevism.

English wasn't even an option for my father in the two-room wooden school house on Kazys Buga Street in Dusetos, now a shoe repair shop.

Another reason my mother spoke the better English was that she wasn't afraid of questioning the meanings of unfamiliar words and phrases. It takes a certain sense of entitlement to expect—*demand*—clarification in a country whose language and customs are not your own. She asked gas station attendants to explain the difference between *juncture* and *junction*. She asked the grocer why milk was labeled *homogenized* when

it was obvious that all milk was the same. She asked me the meaning of
posh and *petulant* and *vitriol*, and what a *prosthetic device* was.

Once, walking down Rush Street, on the way to I don't know where—
what could we have been doing walking down the seedy part of Rush
Street together—she pointed to a sign: "What does that mean?"

"What?"

"Peep show," she said slowly, loud enough so that several people
turned their heads.

I didn't know what to say. How to translate *peep show*?

Several years ago, on a flight to Washington, D.C., where I was to make
a presentation at my first major conference, my mother nudged me as
I was proofing my paper. She pointed to a word in the *Glamour* I had
bought at the airport.

"What does this mean?"

"What?"

"Dildo."

"I'm not going to explain this to you just right now, mother."

"Perhaps I can ask that nice young steward."

"Mom!"

"I'm just kidding."

Although my mother's English was better than my father's, she spoke
to my sister and me in Lithuanian when we were girls. She did this
not only at home, but in public—in stores, on the street—oblivious
to the occasional stares we received from strangers. In this she was different from my father, who insisted on English in the presence of non-
Lithuanians. Once, on a vacation to the Grand Canyon, looking through
the stand-up binoculars where for a dime (back then) you could watch
for a minute or two the very crevices at the bottom, I called to my sister
Rita to come look: *ateik, ateik.*

"Vee cow-moon-ick-ate in English," my father said.

"Are you ashamed of your heritage?" I asked him, in Lithuanian.

"Ah you ashamed of yo con-tree?" he shot back.

43

I mentioned an Ann Landers column about taking pride in speaking one's native language. My father, who read and admired Ann Landers, was nonetheless adamant: *Vee cow-moon-ick-ate in English.*

The irony, of course, was that my father's vocal, overly enunciated English marked him as a foreigner in a way that a quiet, natural Lithuanian would not have. He plowed ahead, oblivious to articles, ignoring the dangers lurking in prepositional phrases. When my American friends would visit, my father would greet them with "How you do?" *How you do, Lisa? Say, Tom, how you do?* After one too many *How you dos*, I couldn't take it anymore. I began to yell: "It's not *How you do?* It's *How do you do? How do you do, dad? How do you do?*"

Although my mother spoke the better English and was not afraid to ask the meanings of words she didn't know, she often insisted on her own interpretations, shrugging away my corrections with a wave of her hand.

"I almost married a business mongrel," she once told me.

"You mean business *mogul.*"

"I could have lived in the lab of luxury."

I envisioned a large white room where well-heeled women mixed vials of precious oils to create Chanel No. 5, where men wearing Armani ties peered under microscopes to examine the inner workings of expensive Swiss watches.

My mother and I are sitting in Jedi's Garden, a restaurant near the Oak Lawn hospital where she has been a regular visitor for the past six months. We switch from English to Lithuanian, interspersing words from one language into another as thoughtlessly as a child baking a cake from two different recipes.

"How are you, mama?"

"My wanes hurt," she tells me, flexing her arm.

"Your John Waynes?"

"The nurse took some blood."

She barely touches her rosemary chicken, plays with the carrots in her vegetable medley.

"Valgyk," I say.

She doesn't eat, but finishes her glass of red wine.

"Another one?"

"No. I don't want people to think I'm some kind of a slush."

As she sees her life closing in on her, her appetite disappearing with each diminishing white cell, my eighty-four-year-old mother relies on memories of the past to keep her grounded in the living. She talks about her mother, whose first language had been Polish, the mother tongue of the Lithuanian nobility. She'd perfected her already fluent Russian in St. Petersburg, where she studied physics and geography. It was at the university, a meeting of the young Lithuanian Socialist League—St. Petersburg Chapter—that she met her future husband, my grandfather, the oldest son of wealthy farmers.

My mother talks about the handsome Frenchman.

"Did I ever tell you the story of the handsome Frenchman?"

"You mean the handsome Frenchman who left his beautiful French girlfriend for plain ol' Aldona Markelis?"

"Yes, that handsome Frenchman. The girlfriend, she really was very beautiful. But also very angry."

"How angry was she, mom?"

"She was so angry she hit me with a shoe."

Most of all, however, she talks about my father, whom she met at a party of raucous Lithuanians on the south side of Chicago in the mid-1950s. She was walking around with a glass of wine in her hand, reciting a poem: "Burn me, like a witch, burn me in blazing fire . . . "—by the revolutionary Lithuanian poet Salomėja Neris.

My father took one look at my mother holding her wine glass as if it were the torch on the Statue of Liberty and fell in love.

It took my mother longer to see the light.

"He's short," were the first words my grandmother uttered when my mother brought him home to meet the family.

But my father bought my mother flowers, and he owned a car, and, besides, at thirty-seven she was not getting any younger.

They never would have met in Lithuania. Or, if by some capricious accident of destiny they had, my mother would have fled to Kaunas at the sight of my grandfather shoveling hog manure, of my grandmother with her babushka muttering from her tattered little book of prayers.

Reading was my parents' strongest bond, the milky glue that helped cement their sometimes tenuous allegiance. They disagreed on money and the principles of child rearing. My father would withdraw into himself, closing like a fist; my mother would cry. Evenings, their bedroom door half open, I would hear voices falling and rising, the rhythmic ta-da, ta-da of Lithuanian sentences, followed sometimes by extended silence, sometimes by laughter.

The waitress comes to check on us.

"Can I take that for you, hon?"

"No. But I would like a *dog bag*."

The waitress smiles.

"I wish I had a camera with me," my mother says.

"Why?"

"To take a photograph of your laugh."

In a minute they're chatting away as if they're soul mates. My mother tells the waitress that she's from Lithuania. The waitress compliments her English and soon discovers that my mother's English was always better than my father's.

"Does anyone ever ask for a cat bag?" my mother wants to know, a reasonable request "because cats need goodies too."

The waitress, who owns a tabby, concurs, but adds that cats are more selective: "Dogs, you can give them anything."

"Yes, dogs are like that," adds my mother. "Our dachshund, Nika, we named her after Nikita Khrushchev, she once grabbed a frozen steak out of the refrigerator when no one was looking."

As my mother pays the bill, the waitress says goodbye.

"Sudiev," my mother answers. Then: "Aufwiedersehen." Finally, for good measure: "Au revoir."

"Have a nice day," I wave.

My words feel flat and lifeless, my farewell as uninspiring as a sack of Lithuanian potatoes.

6C 3914

My sister (*left*) and I with American Santa

Journey to Lithuania

In our Lithuanian neighborhood, Halloween occasioned a flurry of creative badgering for store-bought masks or capes or tiaras. For the costumes to be legitimate, they had to come wrapped in plastic with the words "Made in Taiwan" stamped somewhere on the package. The objects of our greatest desires were wigs: long black Morticia wigs, silky fairy princess wigs, curly orange fright wigs. Every October our mothers nixed the wigs, as well as the flimsy super-hero and fairy princess outfits; we would have to bear the stigma of the home-sewn for yet another year.

We would walk from door to door, dressed as butterflies or court jesters or cats, trudging up and down the block, up and down the steps of two-story brownstones. It was hard work. Some of us, like Diane Metrick, traveled from neighborhood to neighborhood, her parents driving her well outside of Cicero city limits, which we thought unfair, perhaps even illegal. She accumulated more Halloween candy than anyone else, huge shopping bags full that lasted until Christmas.

The battle between my parents and American consumer culture reached its height during Christmas. My parents knew they couldn't simply ignore all of the pernicious American holiday customs. Among their few concessions had been a visit to a department store Santa and additional television viewing time for holiday specials—*Frosty the Snowman, How the Grinch Stole Christmas, Rudolph the Red-Nosed Reindeer.*

My sister and I wanted more, however. Why couldn't we be the proud owners of a dancing, prancing, battery-operated Rudolph? Why couldn't a life-sized plastic Santa decorate our lawn? And why did we always have to get a real tree? Why not one of those pink fakes topped with white acrylic frost? Or a shiny gold tree with branches stiff as broom bristles? Some of the phonies even rotated on their stands, miraculously changing colors every thirty seconds.

Why couldn't we? Why not? The answer was simple. The traditions associated with Christmas in Lithuania were so deeply ingrained that adding to or subtracting from them would have been like fiddling around with the First Amendment. One big difference between us and the *amerikonai* was that our big celebration occurred on Christmas Eve. It commenced with Kūčios, the meal that in Lithuania had always begun with the sighting of the first star. No meat was allowed, and—a much more difficult restriction for the fathers—no alcohol. The table had to be covered with a white linen tablecloth. There had to be twelve dishes. For the twelve apostles, the nuns told us. My sister and I—little accountants—would monitor the evening's procession. We knew that rye bread counted as a dish, but butter did not. I found most of the food unappetizing—pickled herring, pickled whitefish, pickled mushrooms—though a few of the dishes I've grown so accustomed to that Kūčios isn't the same without them: a salad made of chopped beets, peas, navy beans, and celery, smothered in mayonnaise; borscht with mushrooms and potatoes. The meal always ended with *kisielius*, a thick gelatinous cranberry pudding more sour than sweet, followed by *šližikai*, hard little cubes of bread, soaked in poppy-seed milk.

After the Kūčios meal, the opening of presents, or, rather, *present*, for most parents in our neighborhood couldn't afford more than one gift per child (and would have limited the number even if they'd *had* the money). The gift was usually a fairly substantial one—a doll, an appropriate educational game, a chemistry set, a microscope. A sweater or a pair of pajamas might be under the tree as well, though my sister and I didn't count these as actual presents. And one might expect a book or two from grandparents. Once in a while, however, extremely intelligent friends of our parents brought "a little something" that excited us beyond all measure: a Slinky, some Silly Putty.

For the most part, we were satisfied with our new possessions. Occasionally, though, grave errors in judgment were committed by the elders. When I was in fourth grade, I asked for a game called Operation. The object of the game was to remove various organs with a pair of tweezers from a rotund, pasty-looking cardboard patient whose bulbous red nose lit up if the "doctor" accidentally touched a surrounding body part. My mother objected strenuously to Operation, which she had seen advertised on television. She hated the very sight of the cardboard man, his pale skin, his bulging, sickly eyes, his fleshy belly flopping over his corpulent thighs. Instead of Operation, I received a board game called Kelionė į Lietuvą, or Journey to Lithuania. The game consisted of a large dark-green map of Lithuania with a series of penciled-in roads connecting one city of Lithuania to another. Game pieces were not clever little dogs or old-fashioned automobiles, but plastic pyramids. Kelionė į Lietuvą didn't even come in a box; it was simply there, ready to be placed on the kitchen table at a moment's notice, a further indication of its questionable status as a real toy.

Another disappointment occurred the Christmas I was in sixth grade. It was 1969, and Franco Zeffirelli's *Romeo and Juliet* had been released the previous year. Photographs of the two young stars, Leonard Whiting and Olivia Hussey, appeared in every issue of *Teen* and *Tiger Beat*. "A Time for Us," the theme from the movie, played on every radio station in the country. An album was even released, containing brief excerpts of dialogue and some of the famous monologues intertwined with the songs and music. The cover was a little risqué—Juliet gazing into the eyes of her bare-chested Romeo, her nakedness cleverly concealed by her long dark hair—but how could my parents object to Shakespeare? That Christmas Eve I held the magical, record-shaped package for a minute in my trembling hands, then slowly removed the dancing snowmen wrapping paper to find—*Johnny Mathis Sings the Love Theme from Romeo and Juliet.* Other great "hits" on the album included "The Windmills of Your Mind" and "Theme from Love Story." I don't know if my parents ever understood both the safety of their choice and the danger—Mathis's ambivalent sexuality and his soothing, semi-tenor bereft of overt sexual longing contrasted sharply with the songs themselves, so clearly *adult*, suggesting a world of smoky lounges where dispirited men and women attempted to assuage their loneliness and revive their fading youth with dry martinis and meaningless if pleasurable flirtations.

Just when my sister and I thought we were doomed to live lives of abject uncoolness, to be subjected to endless variations of Kelionė į Lietuvą, my parents would turn our little world around and get us what we had hinted at with no real hope of attainment: Mr. Potato Head, Etch-a-Sketch, Twister.

Twister—the game where you "use your bodies as playing pieces"— burst onto the sixties scene promising innocent fun and suggesting lascivious mischief. Television advertisements for Twister depicted a group of well-scrubbed, smiling teenagers sprawled across a big vinyl mat covered with six large circles of color. Players took turns twirling a spinner that indicated which body part was to touch which large dot. The stated objective of Twister was to remain the last person standing.

The commercial's catchy refrain still echoes in my mind:

> Right foot blue! (Clap clap clap.)
> Left hand red! (Clap clap clap.)

For weeks before Christmas I went around the house chanting "Right foot blue! Left hand red!"

"Watt that you singing?" my father asked.

"It's Twister! It's what I want for Christmas!"

"She wants the Twister," I overheard my father say to my mother one evening.

The burst of sunshine that briefly appeared on the horizon of my childhood dreams—the possibility of Twister—was clouded over by the likelihood that my parents would be unable to negotiate the complicated transaction involved in purchasing the game. I wanted to tell my parents "It's just Twister. It's not *the* Twister." I imagined my father going to the toy store and asking for "the Twister," the surly clerk responding that they carried no such item.

1967. Christmas Eve.

We are sitting in the living room, around the tasteful Douglas pine. The presents have been opened. The Vienna Choir Boys are pa-rum-pum-pum-pumming with restraint, the slowest version of "The Little Drummer Boy" on record. My mother is cracking hazelnuts with a sterling silver nutcracker. A visitor, a stranger, a silent man with a deeply tanned face and well-worn pants and a nose as shiny and red as Rudolph's sits next to my father on the brown corduroy sofa. The fact that he speaks not one word of English, that his few words of Lithuanian sound clipped and unnatural, makes me think he does not belong here. The way he downs the shots of vodka my father generously offers although no one else is drinking makes me wish I was someplace else.

According to my father, the man is a sailor. He doesn't look like any sailor I am familiar with, not Popeye the Sailor Man, nor the goofy Gilligan from *Gilligan's Island*.

"Vladas has come to America seeking freedom and a better life," my father continues and recounts the story of the scared and shivering man walking the dilapidated wharfs of the Chicago Port Authority.

"He was looking for *asylum*," my father switches to a slow and pointed English.

"A mental institution?" I am tempted to say.

"Vladas encountered a dock worker who spoke Lithuanian."

"It was a miracle," my mother interrupts.

The dock worker telephoned Dr. Kisielius, who knows every single Lithuanian in the Chicago area. A meeting was called in Dr. Kisielius's basement, responsibilities apportioned: Dr. Kaunas would help find a lawyer, Mr. Baukus would start looking for an apartment, Mrs. Dočkus would provide new clothing, and we, the Markelis family, would have the sailor over for Kūčios.

Why couldn't my father find the lawyer? I want to ask. Or get this guy some new clothes? The sailor man has ruined this special evening, sitting there like a *kelmas*—a bump on a log—oblivious to the shiny red and green and silver ornaments on the tree, the tinsel I had to beg my mother to buy.

"Show him your new game," my father says.

"They don't have Twister in Lithuania," I explain sullenly.

"Yeah, they don't even have Christmas," my sister adds.

"Show him the Twister," my father says firmly.

Not bothering to use the spinner, I angrily announce, "Right foot blue."

As her arms flail about, my sister plants a large stockinged foot onto a blue circle.

It will be years before I wonder what Vladas was thinking as my sister and I twisted amid the gilded wrapping paper, the Choir Boys beseeching us to fall on our knees. Was he picturing Klaipėda, that most international of Lithuanian cities, its streets paved with red brick, its bone-chilling winters, its week of summer—but what a week, with the Baltic warm enough for swimming? Was he contemplating the world he had left behind or the one he was entering, a world of overly heated apartments, a world with a language as tough as Lithuanian meat, a country where children asked and parents gave and gave?

When I ask my mother about the Christmas visitor, she frowns. She claims I'm confusing him with Ponas Senkus, a friend of my father's from the DP days, a thin, bony man who'd been an avid practitioner of yoga. He would lecture my mother, in the gentlest way possible, on the benefits of freshly squeezed carrot juice and the advantages of monthly colonics. Sometimes my sister and I would enter the living room to see him standing on his head. One year he jumped out of a sixth-story window of the downtown Marshall Field's. He survived the fall and sought psychiatric help and continued living as the only white person in all-black Garfield Park where the only Lithuanian to visit him was my father.

Or perhaps, my mother suggests, I'm thinking about the famous Simas Kudirka, who jumped a Soviet cargo freighter seeking political asylum aboard an American Coast Guard ship.

"That's much later, mom."

And besides, what would Simas Kudirka, national hero, be doing at our house? The American shipmen had turned Kudirka back to the Soviets, eliciting a wave of international protest. A television movie starring Alan Arkin as Kudirka was made. We watched the movie; every single Lithuanian in the United States watched the movie, scrutinizing each scene for signs of authentic dialogue and dress.

Suddenly she has a vague recollection of our visitor, but thinks the event occurred during Easter and that the man brought flowers, lilies or daisies.

"It was spring," she says.

"It couldn't have been spring. Rita and I would have long abandoned the Twister."

"The Twister?"

She looks at me as if I've started speaking in tongues.

"Forget about it, mom."

"It was March, or maybe April."

"Whatever you say."

"Do you know that the spring months in Lithuanian are all named after birds? Kovas, balandis, gegužė. Makes sense. In kovas, the rooks begin to nest. In balandis, the doves coo all day long. And in gegužė, well, the cuckoos sing."

I want to make a joke about cuckoos. My mother cocks her ear as if the living room is suddenly full of birds. And I know that whatever I say will be wrong.

Lessons with Profesorius Jakubėnas

Water Reflections

My sister used to go around telling people she was adopted. She explained it this way: "There are hundreds of photographs of baby Daiva, but there are practically none of me." When she was ten, she searched through drawers of family papers for her birth certificate, which my mother had somehow misplaced. Mine, however, was there. The missing certificate was the ultimate proof that she was not the real child of my parents.

There was a deep rivalry between us, a rivalry not uncommon in sisters so close in age—a rivalry exacerbated by the fact that I was, in fact, the favorite, a status conferred at least in part by an accident of nature—I was the oldest child and had the personality that often accompanies the firstborn. No Cicero Public Library librarians turned up at our door asking what *I* had done with the entire series of Let's Learn about Europe books, checked out the previous year. No irate Sisters of St. Casimir called my mother demanding that *I* replace the B+'s on my report card with the original C's. Rita set pigeon traps and brought home stray cats. Her best friends throughout grade school were boys.

From the beginning I did not want her there, intruding upon my perfect life. My mother tells me that on Rita's first birthday, when the guests were in the living room eating *her* cake, and *her* presents were stacked on the coffee table, I stole into the bedroom and climbed into the crib with a pencil with a sharp lead point and attempted to poke out her eyes. Her screams brought forth my horrified mother and saved my sister from certain blindness.

When I was five and Rita three, I told her I knew *all* about Pūkas, the large black feathery creature that lived in our bedroom closet. Pūkas—*fluff* in Lithuanian—had no arms, I explained.

"No mouth, either," I continued, as Rita listened slack-jawed.

"He does have eyes, but they're hidden somewhere beneath all of those feathers, so you don't know when he's looking at you."

"How does Pūkas get about?" my sister asked nervously.

"That's a very good question," I said. "He has claws like a chicken, only smaller. He has tiny chicken feet."

My animosity toward my sister began to dissolve as I realized she could be a useful ally in the ongoing battle against the enemy, in this case, as in most childhood instances, the parents. We both shared the same objectives—more television time, increased allowances, a puppy.

"Other kids are making fun of us because we only get to watch an hour of TV a week," I announced one evening over dinner.

"Yeah, other kids are making fun of us," Rita added.

"Please pass the salt, Aldona," my father said.

I realized that a change in tactics was quickly called for:

"The nuns told us that television is important to our becoming real Americans."

"Yeah. They said that."

My father put down his forkful of sauerkraut.

"We *are* real Americans. What the hell you talkin' about?"

The idea of the allowance was an especially sore point with my father.

"Let me get this straight. We feed you, put the clothes on your backs, and a roof over your heads, and now we have to *pay* you for this great privilege? It seems to me that you should be paying us!"

There was no way around the "allowance," which had a life of its own in our community, creating a domino effect: one Lithuanian child began to receive an allowance, then another, and another. My parents were among the last to give in, protesting that such things were unheard of in Lithuania. They were only somewhat appeased when they realized that allowances had to be earned. We could wash dishes and scour the tub and rake the leaves in the yard.

We had better luck with our request for a puppy. What helped our cause was that back in Lithuania my mother's family had owned a black, short-haired dachshund named Druzhok, *little friend* in Russian. We had seen several photographs of the dignified Druzhok, had been enchanted by his long thin nose, his perpetually alert expression. We had heard of his tragic demise, how the rat poison laid out by the neighbors was never touched by its wily targets. (Years later, my mother changed the story and claimed that the neighbors, envious people, had deliberately poisoned their beloved dachshund.)

"A puppy would pay homage to the memory of Druzhok," I said.

"And protect our family from intruders," Rita added.

And thus it was that Nika, a short-haired, short-tempered dachshund, brown as a squirrel where Druzhok had been a glossy black, entered our lives.

In most cases, naming a family pet is a pleasant activity. Some parents even cede the task to their children. In our family, the process was akin to negotiating Middle East peace. My father believed that a traditional farm dog name was best. My sister and I hoped for something dramatic and glamorous, Ramunė, perhaps, *daisy* in English. My mother, as usual, got her way. She had a talent, a kind of sleight-of-hand that I am still not quite able to fully apprehend, of convincing people that they had an equal voice in a decision at hand, when, in reality, the final say had belonged to her from the very beginning. We'd be at the bakery, selecting the pie for Saturday evening dessert. My sister might suggest blueberry, I might ask for apple. My mother would nod her head and smile: "Blueberry and apple are both fine choices, but what about peach? Have we given a serious thought to peach?"

"Wouldn't it be fun to name the dog after a real person?" my mother announced.

My sister and I eyed each other warily, afraid that we would have to start calling the dog Aldona.

My mother explained that back in Lithuania she and her friends had given each other nicknames, shortened forms of their first names with the addition of the letter *k* at the end. There had been a Duka and an Ika. There had been a Nika as well, though she had emigrated not to the United States like the others, but to England, and was never heard from again.

"I kind of like the sound of Nika," my mother said. "What about you?"

Nika grew up an anxious, unpredictable dog, scared of alarm clocks, yet fearlessly attacking dogs twice her size. I pondered the roots of Nika's neurosis: Nature or nurture? Nurture, I concluded, in the form of Arvydas Žygas, who teased Nika by blowing delicate puffs of air directly in her face. Nurture in the form of my sister, who inflicted her culinary experiments on Nika, the cherries jubilee soaked in cognac, the brownies with nuts she had shaped into smooth little cylinders, then threw to the floor.

"Look, everybody! Nika's eating her own shit!" my sister yelled.

We even took the show on the road, at least on our block, charging a nickel per viewing: Nika, the Shit-Eating Dog.

One of Nika's more perplexing quirks was her aversion to men. We'd know the gender of people at the door by the sounds that Nika made: defiant growls when the visitor was male, barely audible whimpers when the visitor was a female, confused little barks when both sexes were present.

There were two exceptions to Nika's hatred of men. She loved our dad in the inexplicable way that young women sometimes idolize men who greet their affection with casual indifference.

And she adored our piano teacher, Vladas Jakubėnas. When he appeared Saturday afternoons with his bottle-thick glasses, Nika would orbit the living room in little circles of rapture.

Nika was not the only creature who venerated Jakubėnas. Among the Lithuanians of Chicago, he was a celebrity of sorts. A well-known composer in the homeland, he had utilized folk melodies in his lush symphonic pieces, many of which had been performed at the Vilnius Philharmonic. He was our Sibelius, though with his large nose, his big, almost hairless head, and those glasses, he looked more like a living version of the cartoon character Mister Magoo. My sister and I sometimes called him that behind his back, chuckling, although we secretly feared him, feared his anger at our ineptitude, his irritation at our lack of "passion," which mattered as much to him as technique.

"Some coffee, *profesoriau*," my mother would ask when he'd arrive at our house for a lesson. "And perhaps a slice of peach pie?"

Jakubėnas was one of several piano teachers who made the rounds on Saturdays; there was never any shortage of customers. In a neighborhood where not every Lithuanian family owned a television set, a piano was a necessity. Walking the streets of Cicero on a warm spring evening, you could be sure to hear some miserable child mangling the scales, some tone-deaf Aldutė ravaging the simplest of tunes— "Pop Goes the Weasel"—some talentless Jonelis destroying the first movement of Beethoven's *Moonlight* Sonata. Occasionally, though, a player got it right—a passage would seem to play itself, the notes lifting themselves off of the page, lingering in the air like expensive perfume.

My sister and I had already been playing piano for several years when

Jakubėnas appeared in our lives. My mother, who had studied at the Kaunas Conservatory, had been our first teacher. I still remember the *Teaching Little Fingers How to Play* that she kept inside the piano bench, the Thompson books with their yellow covers marking the progression from Grade 1 to 2 to 3.

Throughout the ten years I took lessons, I practiced almost every day, an hour, willingly. I even enjoyed the drills, always beginning with the key of C. In my discipline and dedication I was different from Rita, who preferred almost any other activity to practicing piano. My mother would plead. My mother would threaten. My mother would revoke privileges: "No television during the week."

"You mean you're going to take away the whole whopping hour that we now get?" Rita answered.

She would sit at the piano, grimacing, fidgeting, playing with Nika. "An hour a day," my mother begged. "That's all I ask." Then, "Half an hour a day. That's all I ask." Finally, "Twenty minutes a day." Rita conceded, though sometimes the twenty minutes a day would be clustered into one long marathon session on Friday evening.

For a long time, I was the better player, the one asked to perform in front of company. Then, one year, an earthquake hit my sheltered little world, registering a 4.5 on the scale of human disappointments. Rita surpassed me. I had probably sensed it happening, but had ignored the warning signs: the increasing practice times, the complex pieces she was being given. While she had always been a tall, large-boned girl, she now seemed Amazonian. Her large hands stalked the keyboard.

It was a difficult lesson—that great talent and a little work outweigh a little talent and a lot of work, at least in some areas of life. It was the first time she had excelled at something I did not, a fact I resented. I began to pick fights, telling her that she had been adopted: "Ma and daddy should have taken you back a long time ago. Returned you as defective goods." I made fun of her height. "We'll have to lock her up," I told my mother in my sister's hearing. "She must not be seen by others."

That year Rita moved up to the top of the lineup in Jakubėnas's annual piano recital at the Lithuanian Youth Center, playing the first movement of Beethoven's Sonata *Appassionata*. I was stuck with Debussy's *Water Reflections*. After the concert my mother revealed to me that she had known of Rita's extraordinary talent all along, had known it from the beginning, from Rita's difficult birth.

"I knew that Rita would be a star. That's why I gave her a name that would work just as well in English as in Lithuanian."

At that moment I felt all the love I had for my mother dissipate like droplets of water in a small pond during a prolonged spell of summer heat.

"What did you have in mind for me?" I asked her, thinking of all of the people who had made fun of my Lithuanian name, the kids who'd called me Lady Godiva or, worse, Diver Dan, after the deep-sea diver who fought the villainous Baron Barracuda on the children's show *Ray Rayner and Friends*.

"You? I knew you would be a star as well, but a different kind of star. A star to your husband."

"A star to my husband?"

"Yes. He will be a doctor, or perhaps a professor, a wealthy Lithuanian professor. You will spend your time traveling and reading good books."

I have spent some of my life traveling, and a considerable part of it reading good books. I have done this all without having to resort to marriage to a doctor or a wealthy Lithuanian professor.

My mother is proud of me. She has seen my office at the university, has beamed at the name plate that hangs on the door. (She has also suggested alternate arrangements of my office furniture.) But now that she is sick she cannot travel—I make the three-and-a-half-hour commute to Oak Lawn as often as I can.

"Can't you get a job closer to Chicago?" she asks.

"It's not that easy, mom."

"Can't you be a professor at the University of Chicago?"

"It's the University of Illinois *at* Chicago," I answer, referring to the school that has granted me my doctorate. "And they don't hire their own graduates for tenure-track positions."

My mother wavers between the belief that this is true and a suspicion that I have somehow alienated my professors—by disobeying them, perhaps, or stating my opinion too forcefully.

"You return your library books on time, don't you?" she asks.

"I return them *early*."

"Not like your sister."

"Ma, I think she's gotten better over the course of forty years."

"I'll never forget those librarians at our door. And I still don't think they got their books back."

My parents with Nika, aka Nikita "Stinky" Khrushchev

Visiting Joe Semite

In sixth grade I flunked a geography quiz by claiming Delaware was famous for its corn and Atlanta was the capital of Nevada. My parents, especially my father, began to worry that I was more familiar with the landscape and natural resources of Lithuania than of the United States. I knew that Klaipėda was located on the Baltic Sea, that Lithuanian summers were mild but often rainy, and that vodka was made from potatoes.

Although money was tight, my father decided that a cross-country vacation would not only alleviate my ignorance but also allow the family to experience America's wonders, both natural and manufactured. He mapped out a plan of all the places deemed important to furthering our knowledge of the United States. Several years earlier we had traveled to the East Coast (New York and Maine); this time around, my father decided that, like the gold-miners he had read about as a boy, we would go west. The Grand Canyon, Yosemite, the Petrified Forest, Carlsbad Caverns, the California redwoods, San Francisco, Salt Lake City—these were to be our destinations. We'd stop for a day to visit my mother's cousin in Pasadena, and spend another with a childhood friend of hers in Santa Monica. If there was time, well, then, perhaps Disneyland, perhaps Las Vegas.

Our first stop, however, was Omaha, Nebraska.

"What educational value does Omaha, Nebraska, have for kids?" asked my sister.

"Most people, dey knows the California, and dey knows Rocky Mountains. Omaha, Nebraska? No, not many people knows."

My father, however, *had* known Omaha. It was there that he'd begun to string together the bits and pieces of the language that would have to serve him for almost forty years. It was in Omaha, Nebraska, that he'd befriended several Lithuanians and spent nights drinking Budweiser and discovering other pleasures of American nightlife. Most importantly, it was in Omaha that an elderly priest had given him a job sweeping the floors of the church and the rectory—his first paid work in this new country.

In Omaha, we sat in the car as my father walked up the rectory steps. He wanted to properly thank the priest as well as show him the success that he'd become, what with an attractive wife, two intelligent and reasonably behaved children, an alert brown dachshund, and a blue Ford station wagon. Ten minutes later he walked slowly back, his shoulders bent forward slightly, his eyes narrowed, as if he were squinting, although it was evening and already dark. The priest had died years ago.

I was twelve that summer we headed west in a car smelling of cigarette smoke and dog hair and stale ham sandwiches. The year before I had developed breasts and an attitude that had paralleled their gradual evolution: I was surprised, nervous, increasingly arrogant. My father and I argued in the car, perhaps because I was twelve and had developed breasts. Maybe it was the trip itself that caused his temper to rise so quickly; he had done all of the driving. My mother, like most Lithuanian women in the neighborhood, had never mastered the art of maneuvering an automobile.

We fought over music. Classical stations were clustered around larger cities. As their signals weakened, my father would sigh, turn the radio off, only to turn it on twenty minutes later to Merle Haggard crooning "Together Again" or Glenn Campbell pining for Galveston. It became clear to me that most of the United States listened to country music. What I had not expected was that my father might be among the millions, a convert on the road; he hummed along to "Ring of Fire" and smiled each time "Don't Come Home a' Drinkin' (With Lovin' on Your Mind)" came on the air.

I argued for equal radio time, though I knew that getting my way was about as likely as eating at McDonald's. Still, the idea that I was being deprived of what I saw in sixth grade as my lifeblood—rock and roll—made me determined to argue my case. My father occasionally conceded, allowing me twenty minutes of the Doors, the Stones, and Dylan, then unpredictably putting his foot down on some innocuous soft rock: "If you're going to San Francisco."

"But we *are* going to San Francisco, dad, so why *can't* we play that song?" I protested.

"Wha' kind of a man wears a flower in his hairs?" my father asked.

If my father's admiration for country music was my private humiliation, his public use of English mortified me.

"Excuse please. Vee lookin for exit for Joe Semite," he asked a gas station attendant.

The man looked confused: "Joe Semite?"

"Joe Semite National Park," my dad answered, with growing irritation.

"Da-aad. It's Yo-sem-it-ee," I whispered.

My father also spoke much too loudly, bringing undue attention to the entire family. At a re-creation of the founding of Salt Lake City, a musical extravaganza of heavenly choirs and earthly locusts, a middle-aged couple engaged my parents in conversation.

"We're from California," they said.

"That's nice," said mother. "You must spend a lot of time outdoors."

"Oh, we do, we do spend a lot of time outdoors. We like to play golf."

"*We* like to spend our time going to the theater and reading good books," my mother answered.

"*We* live next door to Arnold Palmer," the husband countered.

"Who is Arnold Palmer?" my father asked.

I sidled to the rear of the crowd. Even I, who hated sports and thought golf a mindless game, knew who Arnold Palmer was.

In the claustrophobic spaces of Carlsbad Caverns, when I told my mother that she was right—I should have worn a sweater—my father announced: "Vee speak de English nau." His words reverberated throughout the cave, bouncing off of the walls. I never felt less American than on that trip, speaking English in public spaces to my immigrant parents.

Other indicators that announced to the world that we were not *real* Americans, but tourists from some backward country, included my mother's refusal to let my sister and me wear t-shirts with peace symbols and my father's habit of introducing himself to people he'd just met.

"My name is Adolfas," he'd say, slowly, as if he wasn't sure whether this was, in fact, the case.

"Adolfas. That's unusual," was a common response.

"In English it's Adolf," my sister would explain. "Like Adolf Hitler."

Even our dog, Nika, marked us as foreigners.

"She's a dachshund," my mother corrected children who dared to call Nika a *hotdog dog*. Sometimes she'd explain that Nika was the shortened form of Nikita, "as in Nikita Khrushchev."

That we had named our dog after the Soviet premier who'd succeeded Stalin and was known for his rehabilitation of political prisoners did not go over well with middle America. Parents would nudge their children and slink away with little embarrassed smiles.

"Yeah, but we call her Stinky," Rita would yell after them.

When we got along, we got along in Lithuanian. My father told riddles in the car: *Pramuši ledą / gausi sidabrą / pramuši sidabrą, gausi auksą.*

"I know that one!" my sister would shriek. "The ice is the egg shell, the egg white is the silver. So, you break through the ice to get to the silver and you break through the silver to get to the gold. The gold is the yolk!"

I rolled my eyes: "Yeah, we only both heard that one when we were three years old."

My sister and I sang songs we had learned at Lithuanian Girl Scout Camp: songs about Lithuanian partisans dying for their country; songs about maidens losing their virginity (never explicit, the lyrics always referred to the picking of the rue); drinking songs.

"You learned *that* at camp?" my father asked, referring to the krambamboli liquor song.

When our voices were strained and our energies sapped, we resorted to a game we played only in the car: Famous Lithuanians. The object of Famous Lithuanians was to name as many well-known people of Lithuanian descent we could think of. They had to have achieved success in a public, English-speaking arena. My parents always won—my sister and I suspected that my mother was loading the deck by including celebrities of questionable Lithuanian ancestry, Walter Cronkite, for example.

"His actual name is probably Kronkitas. Walteris Kronkitas," my mother would say.

Worse, she'd add to the list people we had never heard of.

"You've never heard of John Gielgud?" she'd arch her eyebrows.

"Mom, I'm only in fifth grade," my sister would wail.

"Shouldn't it be Gielgudas?" I'd add sarcastically.

My sister and I would counter by bringing up sports figures. How about Johnny Unitas? Dick Butkus?

My mother, who believed that football was a dangerous and incomprehensible game made up by American men for the sole purpose of befuddling women and immigrants, nonetheless concurred.

"You are correct. Unitas, that's pure Lithuanian. Should be spelled Jonaitis, though. His parents probably were forced to change their names at Ellis Island. And Butkus was Butkevičius, too difficult for ignorant Americans to pronounce."

My father always mentioned Ruta Lee, nee Kilmonaitytė. Lee had appeared in several movies, which none of us had seen, and on episodes of *The Twilight Zone, Wagon Train, Mannix,* and *The Wild, Wild West,* which my parents had never let us watch, fearing their pernicious influence. We knew, however, what Ruta Lee looked like; her photograph often appeared in the Lithuanian daily *Draugas.* It seemed to always be the same picture—same platinum blond hair as fluffy as cotton candy, same slim figure, same perfect white teeth.

At the end of a long day of singing and playing Famous Lithuanians, sometimes interspersed with a few hours of sight-seeing, we could look forward *not* to a restful night's sleep on a comfortable mattress in an air-conditioned room, but a primitive back-to-nature experience in some shower-less campground. The idea of spending money on hotels when we had a perfectly good tent was deemed ludicrous by my father. Skills my sister and I had learned in Lithuanian Girl Scout Camp were put to the test during that long road trip. My father had us pitching the tent, pumping up the air mattresses, fetching water, even collecting firewood. Today I wonder how we all managed to sleep in that one medium-sized tent without killing one another.

My parents came away from our family vacation with a newly found appreciation for the vast natural beauty of the United States: the towering redwoods of California, the intricate mineral formations on the caves at Carlsbad, the sublime expanse of endless ravine at the Grand Canyon.

My sister and I were also not immune to the marvels of nature. For example, we were intrigued by the squirrels that scampered over to the protective stone ledge at the Grand Canyon to feast on peanuts from the hands of tourists.

"You're acting as if you've never seen a squirrel," my mother frowned.

"But these squirrels are *bold-faced*," Rita answered, using the word that the nuns at St. Anthony called students (mostly boys) who veered from showing the proper reverence to those above them in stature (mostly the Sisters of St. Casimir.)

More than the Grand Canyon with its bold-faced squirrels, however, what left indelible marks on our youthful memories were the rest stops / souvenir shops that dotted the highways between every major and minor attraction. Stores filled with rock candy, saltwater taffy, snow globes, silk tasseled pillows with Arizona inscribed in scarlet lettering garnered our complete attention. My sister coveted the tomahawks and bow-and-arrow sets while I craved the faux Native American beaded pendants. My parents allowed one souvenir each for the entire trip, not to exceed five dollars, a policy that plagued us with doubt. What if we bought something in California only to find a better version in Utah?

In general, my sister and I were more in awe of man-made wonders than natural phenomena. The cable cars of San Francisco prompted us to repeat over and over again—until my father threatened to stop the car—"Rice-a-Roni, the San Francisco Treat!" We admired the glittering lights of Las Vegas almost as much as we did our parents' decision to spend good money on a hotel for the night instead of camping. They even decided to gamble for an evening, playing the slots with their hard-earned dollars, an idea that my sister and I greeted with enthusiasm. Not only would we be unsupervised, but stories about my parents winning a million dollars would earn my sister and me untold coolness points among our American friends back home.

We watched television that evening on a small black-and-white set, trying to find a show my mother would disapprove of. We jumped up and down on the beds, and played checkers, and imagined our parents coming back with a million in quarters. How would we lug the money back home? How would we spend it?

My parents returned at one in the morning, down fifty dollars.

I don't know how much my geography improved because of that extended family trip. While I became more aware of location—Arizona and New Mexico were neighbors, after all—I also began to see the country in terms of how different states made me *feel*.

Texas, for example, scared me. Mile after mile of flat dry land came eerily close to the image of Texas I had gotten from watching cartoons. After the initial appeal of cacti dotting the highway wore off, my sister and I began to worry that the car would run out of gas, that we'd sit sweltering in the car as our father walked, then crawled, to the nearest gas station, hundreds of miles away, brushing aside the skulls of long-dead cattle and coyote.

Colorado made me nauseous. As my father drove up and down the winding roads that took us through the Rocky Mountains I sat with my head down between my legs, a bucket nearby, as my sister sat with her face plastered to the car window in disgust.

Utah made me chuckle. I liked the name—"If Ruta Lee lived in Salt Lake City, would she be Utah Lee?" I joked. My father said that the state was full of Mormons, which my sister and I misheard as *morons*. We snickered at all of the morons in one-piece bathing suits as we bobbed up and down in the Great Salt Lake, Nika by our side spitting out water and floating on her back like a meatloaf with paws.

California was where I wanted to live. I was twelve years old, going on sixteen. I wanted to wear flowers in my hair and string together multicolored beads of glass and kiss a long-haired boy on the beach. I could do that in California. California had an ocean and plenty of long-haired boys. Movie stars lived in California, though we hadn't seen any—my parents weren't interested in Hollywood, in Grauman's Chinese Theater or Paramount Studios or even the Hollywood Bowl.

Even the Lithuanians in California seemed different. My mother's pretty cousin was married to a rocket scientist. Their house—a single-family residence, unlike our apartment building—was nestled in a valley surrounded by pretty yellow-pink fog. My mother's Santa Monica friend had studied modern dance. She lived in a Spanish villa with a husband and a daughter and a concrete swimming pool. I knew there weren't many Lithuanians in California, but those who had settled there were better looking and wealthier and possibly even a good deal smarter.

What I loved most about California, however, was Disneyland. It hadn't even been a place I wanted to visit. I was much too sophisticated for amusement parks: I was reading Herman Hesse and listening to Bob Dylan, dreaming about boys and worrying about the size of my thighs. Once I set foot in the Magic Kingdom, however, I was transported to a world where I could momentarily forget the burdens of adolescence. My mother, who turned up her nose at Barbie dolls and television, was shaking hands with Goofy. My father was clapping along at the hoedown at the Golden Horseshoe Corral.

There is a photo of me in Disneyland. I am wearing a red peasant-style dress with white eyelet sleeves. My long straight hair is draped to one side like a golden sash; a dreamy smile spans my face. In so many of the other photos from that time I appear solemn, even churlish. But here I am sitting on a horse on the King Arthur Carrousel. I have spent an hour in the Sleeping Beauty Castle, have ridden a saucer on the Mad Hatter Tea Party ride. I have hummed "It's a small world, after all" again and again. I have tested my courage on the gondolas of Tomorrowland with my sister by my side in mouse ears, my parents below us smiling, real Americans.

Fifth Lithuanian Scout National Jamboree, Camp Rakas, 1968

We Are Always Very Prepared

At Lithuanian Scout Camp I learned the difference between oaks and poplars and maples, though of course we didn't call them oaks and poplars and maples, but *ąžuolai* and *drebulės* and *klevai*. I learned how to extinguish a camp fire properly and how to apply a tourniquet with finesse. I learned what to do if stalked by a bear, though as far as I knew no bears lurked in the forests of Camp Rakas, or anywhere else in Central Michigan. I learned to calculate the distance of a storm by counting the seconds from a rumble of thunder to a flash of lightning.

"Perkūne, dievaiti, nemuški žemaitį," one of our scout leaders said whenever it thundered.

God of Thunder, don't strike down someone from Žemaitija.

She'd finish the rhyme with "Muški guda, kaip šunį rudą."

Rather, strike down a gudas like a brown dog.

I wasn't sure what or who a *gudas* was, though I knew my grand-mother came from the part of Lithuania known as Žemaitija.

This same scout leader told us never to peel the bark off of trees, especially birches: "They scream when you do that."

Lithuanian Scout Camp was real camp, not some YWCA retreat with bunkbeds and air-conditioning. The first day we pitched our own tent, digging a trench around it for water to gather in case of rain. We set up our cots and unrolled our sleeping bags and chose a leader from the six or seven girls who were to be our tent mates. We then proceeded to what was arguably the most important first-day activity of Lithuanian Scout Camp: tent decoration.

We began by clearing off several feet of ground in front of the tent, smoothing over the existing soil with more attractive matter such as sand or mulch. On this patch of earth we spelled out our tent name with twigs and rocks—one year we were the *peteliškės*, or butterflies, another the *vaivos*, or rainbows. Above the name we drew pictures of butterflies or rainbows, sometimes adding the Lithuanian coat-of-arms (a white knight against a red herald) or the fleur-de-lis of international scout-ing at the side. We filled these in with leaves, acorns, moss, branches, pieces of glass, rocks, etc. Finished, we'd admire our work, then trudge through the woods to get to the trough where we washed our faces and hands with cold water and soap, then dried them on two or three damp communal towels.

There were prizes for best decorated tent, given at the end of the two-week period. There were daily commendations for neatest tent and friendliest / most helpful tent and tent that spoke Lithuanian most often—i.e., the tent with girls who spoke Lithuanian most vocally in the presence of scout leaders:

"Man patinka stovykla." *I like camp.*

"Ja. Man irgi." *Yeah, me too.*

In the privacy of our tents we all reverted to the language of American youth, of television and rock and roll and grade school crushes—we couldn't fathom how it was possible to talk about boys in Lithuanian.

Boys, of course, were a central component of the scouting experience. The boys' camp, separated by several miles of forest, was accessible during the hour and a half of *lankymas* allotted after dinner. For the most part, the boys used visiting time to play volleyball or whittle strange little statues out of wood or read *Mad* magazines in the privacy of their tents. The girls, on the other hand, marched bravely in packs of threes and fours into male territory. Once there we stood around chatting with one another, fussing with our hair.

Several evenings a week there were co-ed campfires where a few of the luckier, more sophisticated older girls could be seen sharing blankets with their boyfriends, perhaps holding hands.

I loved the campfires, co-ed or not. I loved the silly skits, takeoffs on fairy tales and Lithuanian legends, satires of scouting life. I loved the way we linked arms while singing *Ateina naktis*—Night is approaching— and wished one another *saldžių sapnų*—sweet dreams—after the song, shouting the words out syllable by syllable: sal-džių sap-nų!

I loved the sound of rain pattering against the tent at night, mysterious and soothing.

I loved the scout leaders. The older ones were like my mother, kind and intelligent, but without the drama. The younger ones were confident and pretty, women I aspired to be one day.

I loved the way we called each other *sese*—Sister. "Can you help me carry this wood, Sese Daiva?" "No problem, Sese Ramune."

I even loved outdoor mass on Sundays, mandatory for everyone except the handful of Lutheran girls whom we regarded with curiosity and a bit of suspicion. We'd march to the makeshift chapel and eye the boys who strummed guitars as we sang a Lithuanian version of "Kumbaya."

Most of all, however, I loved earning badges. I received badges in first aid and forestry and home economics and scouting history. I was envious of girls whose uniform sleeves were covered with the important looking insignias. How could they have possibly amassed such a collection? I failed to get the swimmer's badge—I couldn't dive—but acquired the coveted emblem in knot making. I loved knot making—I admired the perfect simplicity of the square knot and the complex beauty of the hangman's noose.

There were things at Camp Rakas I could have done without, such as all of the ceremony—the raising and lowering of the Lithuanian flag, especially when we had to undergo uniform inspection. A recurring dream: I am at the flag ground, wearing my old olive-green scout uniform; it is too short and much too tight. I have misplaced the red tie or *šlipsas* of the *paukštytės* (Little Birds) and must face the approbation of the slightly older and infinitely more sophisticated scout leaders Rima or Julyte or Lidija.

I could have done without all of the talk about the international principles of scouting as set forth by Lord Baden-Powell, who we knew always wore khaki shorts, even in winter, and donned a hat shaped like a flying saucer. His much younger wife dressed in skirts way below her knees and ugly shoes. The Baden-Powells stressed self-sufficiency and physical, mental, and spiritual development. We knew that the international scouting motto—Be prepared!—meant that we should be in a constant state of readiness, though we weren't sure what we needed to prepare for—snakes, lurking grizzlies, or, perhaps that most dangerous of animals, the huge red Soviet bear engulfing countries like little hives of honey.

"Budėk!" our leader would shout.

"Vis budžiu!" we shouted back with the proper salute—our palms facing outward, our fingertips grazing our foreheads as if we were shielding our eyes from a very bright sun.

What I wasn't prepared for at Camp Rakas were girls who aimed their words like stones at the fragile bones of my psyche. These were not the Cicero girls—the glamorous Alvida Baukus or the caring Audra Gečas or the mischievous Regina Grigaliūnas—but interlopers from tough Chicago neighborhoods. It was rumored that they smoked cigarettes at night behind their tent and let boys leave hickeys on their necks.

"Hey Bugs Bunny," they'd yell across the pavilion where we ate breakfast.

"Well, well, well. Look what we have here," one of them said when I ventured carefully into the chilly water of the lake during swimming hours. "It's Bugs Bunny."

Sometimes they'd pull their upper teeth over their bottom lips and then smack their jaws up and down in unison, producing a fah-fah-fah sound I suppose they imagined beavers made.

Once when we had to form a circle for yet another brainless athletic game and had to hold hands, one of the girls refused to take mine. It hung limply suspended in the air like an undressed puppet. "Fuck you," the girl whispered. I stood there, shocked. Fuck you. I'd often heard the words reverberating through the streets of Cicero, but they had never been directed at me. The fact that they had come from the mouth of a Lithuanian, and a Girl Scout to boot, made the situation unbearable.

That weekend when parents came to visit, my father sensed by my despondent manner that something was wrong. I finally confessed, perhaps thinking that my father would take things into his own hands and complain about the girl to senior counselors, or, better yet, beat her to a screaming pulp of flesh and blood.

Instead, he laughed.

"Da-aad, she said *fuck you.*"

"You should have just said *fuck you* right back to her."

This advice struck me as both mind-bogglingly daring and patently ridiculous. I imagined another, braver self issuing the phrase I had uttered only in my most private fantasies. How could I put forth a confident *fuck you* when I had a difficult time simply saying hello?

I began to think that perhaps Lithuanians weren't always very nice. I couldn't imagine American Girl Scouts saying *fuck you* to one another. It occurred to me that maybe Lithuanian Girl Scouting was different from American Scouting, more like the army. I thought back to an annual meeting of our scouting organization held at the Lithuanian Youth Center in Chicago. We had marched into the main hall in formation, had saluted the flags, had shouted *Vis budžiu!*, when, all of a sudden, a troop of American Girl Scouts appeared, seemingly out of nowhere, to show us their unique scouting customs. We later discovered that they had been invited by our senior leaders to foster goodwill and community building.

The American Girl Scouts weren't wearing olive-green uniforms with navy-blue kneesocks or ill-fitting beige pantyhose, but simple beige skirts and comfortable-looking cotton sweaters. Our visitors sat cross-legged around a pretend campfire in the large hall while we stood around observing as if we were British anthropologists from a bygone era and they the natives of some primitive New Zealand tribe. They sang a song about the importance of keeping old friends, who are like gold, while at the same time making new friends, who are like silver.

We sang songs about flocks of swans flying to Lithuania to defend her from enemies. We sang songs asking God to bless us as he does the birds coming home to nest from faraway places. Many of the songs had been sung by our parents decades ago around campfires in Klaipėda and Telšiai and Utena. Some were folk songs, *dainos*, that had existed long before the printed word had appeared in Lithuania, their melancholy strains and strange, sad lyrics recalling a world where dead relatives and friends materialized in the form of ducks and crows and nightingales. Some of the songs were rousing, even rowdy, suggesting activities way outside the traditional realm of scouting. Others were sung as we marched, their rhythms one with our own lumbering footsteps.

Back then, all those many years ago, I thought I might have enjoyed being an American Girl Scout. Chances are, however, I would have been even more of an outsider with my strange name and parents who spoke in fractured English and didn't know who Mickey Mantle was.

I would have missed the tent-decorating contest and visiting the boys' camp during *lankymas*. Most of all I would have missed the music. Today, when the Lithuanian language seems impossible, a burden of vowels and wayward syntax, the words from some campfire song return as if encoded in the strands of DNA, released by a glimpse of larkspur as I walk in the woods or the sound of rain at night. Sometimes I find myself singing at the top of my voice, suddenly fluent in the tongue of my parents: *Oh you gypsies, where have you come from?* or *Here I stand in silence by the rue garden* or even *Night is approaching.*

::::::::::::::

I have been camping out at my mother's, spending every other weekend sleeping on her living room couch. For these overnight stays, I take along books, my laptop computer, a bagful of Hershey's chocolate Kisses. I sit beside her, book in hand, as she naps or watches Ellen DeGeneres or Oprah or her favorite British comedies on PBS.

"What are you reading?" she asks during a commercial break.

"A book of short stories called *Birds of America*."

"Is it about birds?"

"The title is metaphorical."

She smiles. My mother envisions life in metaphorical terms; we are all birds trying to find our way home, she sometimes says.

She notices another book where I've marked my page by folding back the corner of the leaf.

"You should always use a bookmark," she admonishes.

"I didn't have a bookmark on hand."

"You hurt the pages when you do that."

"Do the pages scream?"

"Don't be silly. They just hurt."

Do they hurt like you? I want to say.

My mother looks like an old tree, her back bent by too many strong winds, her gnarled hands extending to hand me a bookmark like branches reaching out to heaven.

My mother sometimes felt angry in the kitchen

In the Kitchen

The smells I most closely associate with my Lithuanian childhood consist of whiskey and cigarette smoke and Chanel No. 5, a Christmas present to my mother when money wasn't tight. My father kept referring to it as Channel No. 5: "I bought your mother a television station," he'd say. It had gotten a laugh, and quickly became fixed in his limited repertoire of jokes in English, like his running gag concerning hamlets and omelets. He had once opined to a group of fellow engineers that it seemed to him that young women in the United States had difficult life choices to make. "Between higher education and early marriage," he'd said solemnly. "Between Hamlet and Omelet."

My mother borrowed and made her own this particular take on words.

"Who wants Hamlets?" she'd ask Saturday mornings, spatula in hand, ready to add chopped ham to the thick layer of beaten egg on the skillet.

She was always mangling the English language, intentionally or not.

"Time to pay the trolls," she'd announce whenever my father pulled up to an interstate "troll booth."

I imagined his hard-earned quarters going to keep some unseen monsters satisfied.

Another time, admiring a neighbor's garden, my mother pointed to a row of hardy red flowers and declared, "What lovely craniums!"

I ask friends to name their favorite childhood aromas; their answers make me jealous: freshly baked bread, apple pie, potato pancakes. I wonder why my olfactory memories don't include home cooking since my mother was a good cook—she took pride in the meals she managed to concoct for us night after night, made with fresh ingredients, balanced and nutritious. Like other Lithuanian moms in the neighborhood, she refused to avail herself of convenience foods; TV dinners were out of the question, an abomination of the highest American order. Soups were always made from scratch: pureed carrot, beef barley, vegetable. In winters there was borscht, heavy with mushrooms and potatoes, served with a heavy dollop of sour cream. Summers we enjoyed cold beet soup, pink as the American Beauty roses in Mrs. Skruodys's garden, sprinkled with dill and green onion, garnished with bits of boiled egg.

For the most part, I'd finish everything on my plate. Exceptions included *balandėliai*—little doves—which we often had for dinner. They weren't really birds, but egg-shaped croquettes of pork entwined in translucent layers of cabbage held together by bits of string. Pigs-in-a-blanket, an American friend called them, a marginally more acceptable name than little doves. I was reluctant to eat *balandėliai*, just as I resisted *kiškis*, despite my mother's reassurances that we were dining on meatloaf and not Bugs Bunny.

Although my mother was proficient in the kitchen, she often seemed a reluctant cook. I remember her sighing loudly as she peeled potatoes or stirred the soup.

"Mom, why doesn't daddy ever make dinner?" my sister once asked in his presence.

"Why don't *you* ever make dinner?" he asked with annoyance.

"Because I'm only eight years old."

She was dismissive of women who obsessively clipped recipes from magazines, who asked for appliances for Christmas, large and clumsy *kugelis*-makers that grated seven potatoes at a time, who spent Saturdays baking elaborate frosted tortes for Sunday after-church gatherings. Her cookbook collection consisted of a nameless tome whose cover had faded to impressionistic depictions of roast chickens and baked apples, as if Monet had done the illustrations.

While other Lithuanian mothers carefully instructed their daughters in the basics of cooking, my mother shooed us out of the kitchen. She refused to buy me an Easy Bake Oven for my eighth birthday despite my constant *prašau prašaus*, getting instead a lavish picture book entitled *France and Its Peoples*. By the time I was in high school I had read *War and Peace* (at least the peace parts). I could play a halfway decent game of chess and stumble through Debussy's *Water Reflections* on the piano. But I had no idea how to roast a chicken or baste a turkey or even chop an onion.

"She'll learn to cook when she has to," my mother would tell my father, who felt that there was something terribly wrong with this scenario, though he himself couldn't mash a potato.

My ineptitude came to the fore most clearly the day my mother had an unexpected library board meeting and Rita was practicing with the high school orchestra. My mother had prepared spaghetti sauce beforehand and had measured enough pasta for the meal. The sauce had to be heated up, the spaghetti cooked. Heating the meat was easy compared to the process involved with the spaghetti. I let the water boil, as my mother had instructed, then dipped the spaghetti in and out of the pot, slowly, like a washerwoman doing laundry in an old-fashioned tub.

"Maybe it's supposed to taste that way," I said to my father, commenting on the crunchiness.

"Maybe," said my father.

Throughout most of my twenties, I survived on gourmet frozen dinners and Chinese take-out and bagels with a variety of toppings. Oh, there was the occasional tin of muffins, baked with twice the sugar recommended by the *New York Times Cookbook*, bought with the mistaken belief that a cookbook can make one a cook. When I was feeling especially ambitious, I'd scramble up some eggs.

My first husband loved to cook. I cleaned the house and did the laundry and always washed the dishes. At times I tried a little culinary experimentation and concocted what I thought was a suitable meal. My ex objected to my presence in the kitchen, confirming my suspicions that cooking could be a battleground for issues much deeper than whether there was enough salt in the stew. He resented my attempt at apple dumplings. He disapproved of the way I made Swedish meatballs.

"Firmer. You have to make them firmer," he'd say, grabbing the meat from my hand, rolling it into angry little balls.

He'd sigh in disgust. "Your mother never taught you anything."

This is not, strictly speaking, true.

My mother taught me how to make birds, graceful cranes, from little pieces of paper. She taught me to recite from memory, with perfect Lithuanian precision, all twelve verses of the children's classic *Meškiukas Rudnosiukas* when I was only three. She taught me to avoid heavy, sweet-smelling cologne—"You don't want people fainting all around you"—and to stand up straight, because "Tall women have more fun."

It strikes me now that my mother had associated meal preparation with a strict partition of gender roles; she had wanted to break out of this domestic penitentiary, but it was impossible, or nearly so, for an immigrant woman in her forties to leave behind that which was so firmly engrained in the collective female psyche.

As a young woman growing up in Lithuania, she had wanted to be an architect. My grandmother told her that this was not a proper profession for women, so my mother read Goethe and Heine and went to the university in Bonn to further her study of German literature. One day in the late 1930s the provost called her in and told her that she would have to leave. He was sorry, sincerely sorry, she was such a good student and her German was so good she had everyone fooled, but someone had brought to his attention that Valaitis was not a German name.

Here in the United States she thought she might try interior design. She attended Northwestern for a year and was told by the director of the program that she had talent— "true" talent, my mother would stress. But classes were expensive, and then I came along.

"Don't ever have children," my mother told me more than once.

Perhaps her refusal to teach me to cook was a form of rebellion, a way to show the Lithuanian world that I was meant for better things.

She'll learn when she has to.

∘∘∘∘∘∘∘∘∘∘∘∘∘

In my mother's refrigerator there is cranberry juice and buttermilk and French bread and cottage cheese and Little Debbie Nutty Bars. There is a carton of blueberries and a container of homemade chicken soup. There is sliced ham from Bobek's delicatessen and carefully wrapped leftovers from yesterday's meal for one—chicken with mushrooms, mashed potatoes. There are apples and bananas and dried apricots and little mounds of chocolate wrapped in golden foil.

What good is all this food, I think, when she has no appetite?

Perhaps my irritation stems from guilt. I would like to feed her, to cook for her, to nurture her back to the semblance of the woman she was just a few years back. But she eats only what Irutė, her care-taker and friend, prepares for her. The fact that I have shown up with a McDonald's milkshake, vanilla, as my mother requested, makes me feel as if I've failed her in some substantial way.

"Oh, this is much too big," she says and takes a reluctant sip.

The apartment smells of Lysol and valerian drops. A basket of bright pink azaleas stands in front of the picture window, arrogant in their optimism.

I bend down to take a sniff.

"Azaleas don't smell, honey," my mother informs me.

She takes another sip of her milkshake and points to some books on the glass coffee table: "Those are for you."

She has been giving away her books, stack by little stack, sometimes grouped according to theme. I see a picture book of old Lithuanian churches, another of traditional Lithuanian costumes.

"Don't you have any Lithuanian cookbooks?"

"Cookbooks?" she asks, as if I've uttered a particularly distasteful word.

"I'd like to learn to make something authentically Lithuanian."

"Like what?"

"Oh, I don't know. Potato pancakes," I say.

"Those are Jewish. Jews have been eating latkes for centuries."

"Cepelinai, then."

"You don't really want to learn to make cepelinai," she says firmly, referring to the potato-covered meatballs we'd smother with sour cream and bacon.

"What's left?" I ask.

"Little doves."

"I hate little doves."

She laughs.

"You were always a fussy eater," she says, then adds: "And not much interested in cooking."

The unveiling of the Picasso, 1967. Courtesy of *Chicago Sun-Times*.

Chicago

My parents believed that one way to contain the flood of popular American culture was to construct a dam out of the lofty bricks of European civilization. If they couldn't prevent my sister and me from playing Mother-May-I in the alleys of Cicero with questionable non-Lithuanian friends, if they couldn't thwart the growing pile of comics in our bedroom, well, then, they could take us to museums and expose us to great books and magnificent architecture and classical music.

"We're going to the *meno institutas*," my mother announced one Saturday morning in July when I was ten, her voice an unconvincing whisper of excitement.

My sister and I didn't want to "visit the pictures" at the Art Institute; we wanted to ride the Candy Cane Sleigh at Santa's Village Amusement Park and see the Twirling Snowballs and feed the reindeer with Diane Metrick.

"Reindeer bite," my mother explained in Lithuanian. "You'll get rabies."

"Cos too much," my father continued in English, as if the switch to the language my sister and I spoke with ease would strengthen the firmness of his message. "An too far," he added, as if Santa's Village was in another country.

"It's only an hour away," we whined.

"Vie go distan suburb? Vee explore gray seedy of Chikaago."

"It's *great city*, dad," I muttered.

"Yeah, learn to speak English," my sister added.

"No Satan's Villa for you," my father answered, repeating the phrase several times.

And so instead of piling into the Metricks's beige sedan, we boarded the Douglas L on Cicero Avenue, my mother clutching her handbag, my sister and I in prim little cotton dresses, my dad in a short-sleeved shirt. As the L climbed to the level of the treetops, rumbling slowly downtown, I felt a growing sense of excitement. Although the day was hot and there was no air-conditioning on the trains, the breeze at the open window felt good. And I liked the way the conductor called out the names of the stops, stressing one syllable over the rest: Killl-dare, Pu-laaas-ki, Central Paaa-rk.

"We're in sunny California," my sister shouted as the train stopped at Twenty-Sixth and California, near the Sheriff's Office and the Cook Country Jail. A grizzled old man entered clutching a paper bag next to his chest; a group of black teenagers smacking gum grabbed the handrail above my father's seat. My mother held her purse a little tighter. A few stops later, the L descended underground into total darkness. We stepped out at Adams holding hands, looking around to catch our bearings. We trudged up the large concrete stairs, my sister and I, *step-step-rest, step-step-rest*, emerging into the bright sunlight of day.

Inside the Art Institute, room led into high-ceilinged room like a maze. We spent an hour with the Rembrandts and Vermeers, my mother reading each title aloud. She then steered us toward the Impressionists, talking all the time as if she owned the pictures, then on to modern European art. Rita, prone to nightmares, began to whimper at Dalí's *Inventions of the Monsters*. My mother, worried that my sister would have a nervous breakdown right then and there, decided on a quick change of venue: "We're going to see the Africans and Greeks." She said she wanted us to envision the world as a place made beautiful by the hands of *ordinary* people. *Liaudé*, she said. The folk.

I stared at a giant warrior mask with teeth as protruding as my own while Rita shrunk away from the disembodied head of a female deity carved out of stone.

Later that week my sister and I demanded that my mother turn our apartment into a museum. We pestered her to tape our tempera-painted pictures onto the living and dining room walls, in the kitchen, even the bedrooms. My father came home from work to find the house filled with our creations: pastures full of swaying flowers and trees with apples as big as bowling balls; oceans swarming with ruby-colored fish; little girls with huge bows in their hair, girls who towered over their tiny mothers and even smaller fathers.

We were soon whining about amusement parks again.

"Can we go to Riverview? All our friends have been to Riverview."

"You'll fall off the Ferris wheel," my mother said, inculcating yet another lifelong phobia.

"No Reeferview for you," my father answered, repeating the phrase over and over with self-satisfaction.

Instead we went to the opera, the Lyric Opera production of *Boris Godunov*. We didn't understand why our parents were so thrilled to be here, listening to music in Russian—a language I thought they had hated—with action that took place in the 1500s, mostly in monastery basements. The initial pleasure of peering down from on high and viewing the people at the bottom soon wore off, as did the fun in my sister's loud insistence that the opera should have been named Boris Badenov after our favorite cartoon villain, the Pottsylvanian spy whose schemes of killing "moose and squirrel" we constantly booed.

"He's the world's greatest no-goodnik," Rita announced as the curtain rose on Act I.

"Sharrup you mouth," I couldn't resist, mimicking Boris's favorite response to his sidekick Natasha.

There were more trips downtown, to the symphony once or twice, to the Natural History Museum, to the Chicago Public Library. We went to the unveiling of the Picasso at the Daley Plaza. The place was packed: there were men in business suits and polyester ties; women in pencil skirts and heels and crisp white blouses, coifed hair held in place by Aqua Net; old people who couldn't hear when you said "Excuse me" and had brought folding chairs as if this were a picnic. But there were also teenagers in jeans and sandals and long straight hair. A few young men and women were handing out pamphlets protesting the Vietnam War; for the most part, they were ignored.

Mayor Daley talked about the great gift the city had received from *Pick-ass-o*. "What is strange to us today will be familiar tomorrow," he read slowly from a piece of paper. He then pulled a heavy tasseled cord: the blue cloth covering of the statue collapsed to the ground to expose an enormous steel creature with giant wings and a small, odd, angular face that reminded me of the countenance of one of the nuns at school.

"What's it supposed to be?" people murmured.

"An aardvark."

"An angel."

"It's a girl. Dats what da sculpture said," a woman wearing a large orange hat and oversized sunglasses proclaimed.

I knew the difference between *sculpture* and *sculptor*, but I dared not correct the woman. I had seen what happened when my impetuous mother did this: People cast her dirty looks or sometimes even told her to mind her own business. My mother shoved us away from the woman as if she were a criminal, then whispered: "It can be anything you want it to be."

"It's the god of birds," my sister shouted. "Look at the pigeons worshipping at its feet."

A man behind us wearing a suit complained: "Dey shoulda builda stat-chew ta hahnor a great poizon from Illanoiz. Like Abe Lincoln."

"Or Ernie Banks," another man suggested.

"Who's Ernie Banks?" my mother asked.

"Ernie Banks?" The man looked outraged. "The baseball player?"

"Does he play for the Cubes?" my father asked helpfully.

I wanted to crawl away in shame. I knew almost nothing about baseball, but I knew who Ernie Banks was. Non-Lithuanian classmates whispered his name like a god's. My feelings of embarrassment were coupled with a sense of pity for the man who'd suggested the Ernie Banks statute; clearly, he lacked imagination. Still, I wished that my parents were just a little more worldly. My mother thought Wrigley Field (or Wrigley Field's as she called it) was a department store, the poorer cousin of Marshall Field's. My father refused to let us go to the Odditorium, the Ripley's Believe It or Not Museum in Old Town, even though I told him it was like the Art Institute in some ways, filled with artifacts: ossified human heads and sharks' teeth as big as chainsaws and a sculpture of JFK made entirely of gum balls.

"Seeing is believing," I told my father, mimicking the Ripley's motto.

"Living is believing," my father answered, once again taking a popular slogan and turning it upside down so it made both perfect sense and no sense at all.

As far as my parents were concerned, there was no need to venture beyond the borders of the charted landscape—the North Side offered nothing in terms of necessity or luxury. In their parochial outlook—at least when it came to the city's geography—my parents were no different than other members of the Lithuanian community, who bought their bread from Baltic Bakery and their cars from Balzekas Motors, who married off their sons and daughters at the Lithuanian Youth Center and buried their dead in St. Casimir's Cemetery.

My parents' disinterest in what lay north of the John Hancock Tower on Michigan Avenue wouldn't have bothered me so much had it not been for Old Town, home not only to Ripley's Believe It or Not but to a store called the Bizarre Bazaar that carried ankle bells and glow-in-the-dark posters and strawberry incense and little soaps that smelled like tomatoes. I was verging on adolescence; my desire for Flower Power patches for my jeans coincided with a growing need to break away from the old-fashioned, constricting world of my parents. I wanted to listen to folk music at the Quiet Knight or the Earl of Old Town while puffing on a cigarette, perhaps talking to a member of the Chicago Seven, whose trial I had watched on television. I knew which side I was on from the very beginning: the hippie defendants were young and smart and hip and looked as if they were having fun.

The first time I set foot on Chicago's North Side I was fifteen. I had persuaded Cindy Zikowski to cut school and take the L to Old Town one spring afternoon.

"We can catch an afternoon concert at the Earl," I said casually, as if I'd done this many times before.

Cindy and I were friends from theater arts. We were smart and shy and well developed, though Cindy was smarter and shyer and bustier than I. Rumors circulated concerning her bra size—40D, the boys whispered. An even greater burden was her almost supernatural intelligence; she had the highest IQ in all of Morton East, 192, higher even than Harold Smith's, president of the Chess Club.

We wore our most tattered bell-bottom jeans. I donned a red wool poncho while Cindy put on a fringed leather jacket. We piled on the makeup—orange eye shadow, frosted lipstick, globs of Maybelline mascara—and dabbed patchouli oil behind our ears.

As we sat in our seats on the L, clutching our clove cigarettes, I remembered the day my family rode downtown to the Art Institute, visitors from Squaresville, Lithuania. I thought of how far I'd come, how unutterably cool I looked.

Strolling down Wells Street, Cindy and I struggled to maintain our facades of practiced indifference. Everything was fascinating: brass hookahs and multihued rolling papers in the windows of little shops,

Hare Krishnas selling incense sticks, a young male couple walking hand-in-hand.

"Far out," Cindy would say when she saw something particularly interesting.

"Yeah, man," I'd add.

A white banner waving in the wind announced the Earl of Old Town. We entered with trepidation; it was much easier to be noticed in a cozy, storefront place where everyone seemed to know everyone else than in a bigger, more impersonal club. Cindy and I were worried that the tall, somewhat surly looking man at the cash register, who turned out to be owner Earl Pionke, would look deeply into our faces and ask in a very loud voice "Can I see some identification?"

We sighed in relief as he smiled and led us to a round table toward the back of the room. We didn't dare order alcohol, however; how embarrassing it would have been to have our cover blown surrounded by long-haired women in cottony flower dresses and leather boots and bearded men in overalls who might have been folk singers themselves. We pretended to admire the bare brick walls while secretly scanning the place for stars of the Chicago folk scene like Steve Goodman and Bonnie Koloc.

The musician that afternoon was the Autoharp player Bryan Bowers. We weren't exactly sure what an Autoharp was—it looked suspiciously like the *kanklės* played by young girls in Lithuanian costumes at somber independence day commemorations. The minute Bowers started performing, however, we relaxed, charmed by the music and Bowers's easy manner with the audience.

We clapped along to "Pick a Bale of Cotton" and listened in respectful silence to "The Battle Hymn of the Republic." We smiled at "Twinkle, Twinkle Little Star," and strained to listen to new, unfamiliar songs about love and longing. I suppose we would have preferred a more hard-edged performer, one brimming with discontent, but we were glad just to be there, in Old Town, listening to folk music. Everything was going well until the end of the concert, when Bowers announced: "I'd like to conclude with "Will the Circle Be Unbroken?" Take your neighbor's hand in yours and sing along."

There were men on both sides of us. I had never held the hand of a boy. Cindy had never held the hand of a stranger. I played with the beads on my macramé purse; Cindy fiddled with the ice cubes in her Diet 7-Up.

"Come on, everybody, hold hands," Bowers repeated and began to sing. He stopped in the middle of the song. "You two," he shouted out and pointed to us for all the audience to see. "Don't be shy. Take the hand of your brother."

"Will the circle be unbroken," we sang, our hands limp and clammy, our voices shy, humiliated echoes of our former selves.

The ride on the L back home seemed endless. We were stuck in the tunnel between Clinton and LaSalle for fifteen minutes. The train's dim indoor light did little to illuminate the passengers, who seemed like cartoon ghosts of themselves, faces tinged in gray.

"You're a little late for dinner," my father said.

"The meatloaf is cold," my mother added.

"How come you're wearing all that makeup?" Rita asked. "You look like a slut."

"Shush," my mother admonished, though I could see she was upset.

"I had to stay after school to work on a project," I lied.

"What kind of project?"

"An art project."

I wasn't even taking art that semester, but my parents didn't know that. If I'd had said history or geography or English, they would have asked questions: What period of history? What part of the world? What novel, what poem? But art was large and uncertain and imprecise. Art was anything you wanted it to be.

Arvid (*far right*) and his female followers

Looking Homeward

We moved one more time, when I was in sixth grade, to a sturdy brick building half a mile south, the other, better side of the tracks. We moved on Thanksgiving Day—I'm still not sure how my father got movers. As we spent the day unpacking boxes, my mother directing the placement of things the way she directed everything else in our lives—firmly, sure of her superior taste and the rightness of her ways—a sign of the future possibilities of my new life manifested itself. In the middle of planning everything, my mother had forgotten dinner. My father suggested a trip to Sawa's Old Warsaw smorgasbord, in itself noteworthy—restaurant meals were as rare as raises in allowance. My mother, however, did something better. She ordered a pizza. My parents had never, in their entire immigrant lives, ordered pizza. For my mother pizza was an English muffin with ketchup and a slice of mozzarella cheese, slightly broiled, and sprinkled with oregano. The taste of that Thanksgiving pizza, extra large with sausage and mushrooms, the cheese so heavy I thought it might drown, still lingers in my mouth. We sat in the living room, eating out of the box, and all I could think of was how envious classmates would be when they discovered how I spent my Thanksgiving. I pitied them, at home with their elaborate turkey dinners.

Our new residence was a multi-flat, a clear sign that my parents had, once again, moved up in the world. We now collected rent from *four* tenants—Mr. Chainauskas and his elderly mother; Macy and his wife, whose name I can't even remember, so diminished was she compared to her volatile husband; drunken Ted; sinister Mario. My sister and I ignored them—we owned the place, after all—though it was hard to avoid Ted, who was retired and lived in the basement and appeared whenever I did the laundry, asking me whether I had a boyfriend, telling me I should be in the movies.

Although my parents extolled the benefits of our new home on a regular basis, I didn't like that the building took up an entire corner lot, as if we were wealthy landowners whose servants lived in the smaller two-flat brownstones down the street. I wanted to be a sixth-grade aristocrat without looking too much like one. Another drawback—winter evenings the radiators not so much hissed as sizzled, coming to life at inexplicable moments.

"Listen, the elves are frying bacon again," I'd tell my sister over and over as she tried to do her homework.

"Cut it out."

"Sizzle sizzle sizzle."

She'd finally move into the little porch that my parents had converted into her bedroom. She was happy with the room, its unimpeded view of the garden and, more important, all back alley shenanigans. She was even happier when my mother told us that *my* new bedroom had belonged to the previous owners' only daughter, who had died of a childhood illness.

"Probably under mysterious circumstances," said my sister. "At the age of eleven."

In order to lift the spell of underlying gloom, I painted my bedroom canary yellow and talked my mother into papering one of the walls a burnt-orange and dark-yellow Aztec print. I convinced her to let me cover the floor in an orange-and-yellow deep shag carpet. As if all this yellow and orange wasn't enough to brighten both my bedroom and my outlook on life, I hung a framed poster of Van Gogh's *Sunflowers* above my bed.

My new life proved to be less than sunny. My previous hope—that the new address would allow others to perceive me in a different light, that popular girls who had eschewed my friendship would now gravitate toward me—never materialized. To make matters worse, I was, by some karmic misunderstanding, some grand cosmic mix-up, the next-door neighbor of Arvydas Žygas, my nemesis since second grade. Even more irritating was the fact that he had become an object of feminine adoration—every single female in the universe seemed to love him. Except me. The nuns loved him. He stayed after school to clean their erasers, expertly clapping them together to free them of dust as he talked about the priesthood. Mothers loved him. He blessed their bologna sandwiches—in Lithuanian—before wolfing them down with lemonade.

I was doubtful of Arvid's "call" to a religious life, suspecting that underneath a veneer of do-gooder gallantry beat a heart of immeasurable darkness. He had enchanted the Sisters of St. Casimir, who in class had extolled the paths of the priest- and sisterhood open only to God's elite: "Many are called, but few, *few* are chosen." And he had captivated the sixth-grade girls with his unthreatening appearance, his fluffy blond hair and round baby face.

"You look like an overgrown chick," I told him over the fence.

"At least I'm not a Big Buck," he answered, referring to the name he'd given me because of my protruding teeth.

For the next year or so Arvid would fling various objects at my bedroom window, wisely choosing a time when my parents weren't home. He threw rocks in the summer, rocks covered with snow in the winter. One Fourth of July he lobbed a firecracker that rocketed straight through the window, spiraled across my bedroom, and landed in the kitchen, exploding an inch away from the refrigerator.

Once I came to the window, disturbed, yet again, by the thwack of stone against glass, to see Arvid accompanied by Arthur, our resident neighborhood delinquent. Sticking through the opening of Arthur's pants was a hotdog. I gazed in open-mouthed disgust when he suddenly yanked it off, an expression of mock horror on his face. Arvid waved his hand back and forth, a smile on his face like a contestant's in a beauty pageant. I was enraged. This was not something I could complain about to my parents—the topic was just too sensitive.

The one beacon in the hopelessly murky waters of sixth grade was Sister Gracilda. I loved Sister Gracilda. She was not young—her face was deeply lined, and a shock of gray hair peeped through her headpiece. But she understood the burgeoning idealism of adolescents, the social and political concerns we were just beginning to grasp. In class we discussed the Vietnam War, women's rights, the environment.

"What can be done about waste?" she once asked, slowly surveying the room, stopping here and there to examine a face, as if one of us sixth graders might possibly be clever enough to offer a workable solution.

"I suppose we could burn it," Jonas Žibutis answered.

Sister patiently explained that toxins would be released into the air, thus adding to the even more significant problem of air pollution.

"We could bury the garbage in big holes," suggested Felicija Radvilas.

"And we could make convicts do the digging," Raimundas Mičiulis added.

Getting convicts to do the labor was a popular solution among sixth graders.

We explored the possibility of seepage. Following Sister's lead, the majority of the students believed that garbage could filter through the soil and might eventually rise to the top, greatly inconveniencing the lives of the people in the surrounding area. A few holdouts remained convinced that garbage did *not* have a life of its own—once dumped, it stayed dumped.

I raised my hand timidly.

"Maybe we could place the garbage in large plastic containers and then lower the containers into the ocean."

A voice from the back of the classroom exploded in scorn: "That's the stupidest thing I've ever heard."

"What's your brilliant solution, Arvid?" I countered.

"Of course, we could just be more careful to begin with," Sister Gracilda said diplomatically. "We could recycle wrapping paper. We could drink out of mugs and not paper cups. We could donate our clothes to the poor instead of throwing them in the garbage."

We nodded wisely, as if we had been thinking of this all along, but had just somehow forgotten to express it.

It was in Sister Gracilda's class that my enjoyment of reading blossomed into a full-fledged obsession. For several years I had been an avid, methodical reader of formula fiction, mainly horse books and Nancy Drew mysteries. The horse books had in common the underlying theme of living out one's destiny, which in equine terms meant running very quickly and rescuing good people from danger. Similarly, Nancy Drew always did what she had to do in order to save the day. The books always began the same way—with warnings to Nancy in the form of unsigned letters or veiled telephone calls not to go to Pine Hill or Moonstone Castle. Perhaps I identified with Nancy in this respect—my mother was always telling me not to drive my bike too far or eat too fast or read too late into the night.

Sister Gracilda urged us to expand our perspectives, to read newspapers, magazines, and books about history. She recommended novels—*The Island of the Blue Dolphins*, *The Witch of Blackbird Pond*, *A Wrinkle in Time*. She managed to extract from our mandatory sixth-grade reader those selections that we might actually enjoy, such as James Thurber's "The Dog That Bit People" and "The Night the Bed Fell." I laughed so hard that my mother had to ask me what the matter was.

Perhaps jealous of Sister Gracilda's growing literary influence, my mother suggested books she had loved at different stages of her life: *The*

Red Pony, A Tree Grows in Brooklyn, Madame Bovary, and *Gone with the Wind,* which she'd read in a hospital bed in Germany during the war, suffering from typhus. Dying from typhus, according to my mother. She often recounted her return-from-the-dead experience, complete with dark tunnel, flashing lights, and heavenly music.

"And Herman Hesse. You'll like Hesse," she told me, "although, of course, he should be read in German."

I trudged over to the Cicero Public Library on Cermak Avenue and asked where the English-language Hesses were kept.

"Those are in the *adult* section," the ancient librarian told me. Her look suggested it'd be years before I'd be allowed to even touch a book in that hallowed area.

On my next trip to the library I loaded up on four or five adolescent books, inserting between them a copy of *Steppenwolf,* whose Dewey decimal number I found simply by thumbing through the adult card catalogs. The withered librarian said nothing. Another time I slipped *Madame Bovary* between *My Side of the Mountain* and *The Little Prince.*

I stopped reading *Madame Bovary* after ten pages—not enough action. In sixth grade I was still buying comic books, though I'd begun to supplement my standard Archie fare with Classic Comic renditions of Shakespeare plays. I still remember a voluptuous, scantily clad Helena chasing a strong-jawed Demetrius through the woods, an image I returned to again and again for the sensual pleasure it gave me.

More than comic books, however, I loved magazines. Weekly allowance in hand, I'd browse through the latest arrivals at the seedy drugstore on Cicero Avenue. *Teen, Tiger Beat,* and *16* eventually gave way to *Seventeen* and *Mademoiselle* and sometimes *Glamour.* I especially liked the fall college issues showing glossy-haired co-eds in nubby wool sweaters and penny loafers strolling to classes as colorful leaves skittered across expansive lawns.

My mother was wary of the magazines—*Seventeen* for a twelve-year-old?—but the advice contained between their covers, at least in the sixties, was innocuous enough not to raise too many red flags. The magazines commended friendliness, good citizenship, and impeccable personal grooming. The ideal young woman was college bound, listened respectfully to her parents (even if she disagreed with their opinions), and used the appropriate beauty and hygiene products to enhance her natural attractiveness.

Only once had my mother threatened to nix my magazine-reading habit. In her secret bimonthly inspection of my room, she'd come up with a suspicious entity she was sure I'd been brainwashed into buying.

"What is *this*?" she demanded, holding a tube labeled Neat in front of my face as if it were a stick of dynamite.

"It's a depilatory cream."

"A what?"

"A cream to take hair off my legs."

"What's wrong with the hair on your legs?" she asked.

It was no use arguing with my mother. In our neighborhood, you could tell the women who had emigrated from Lithuania from those who'd been in the United States for a generation or two—the former never shaved their legs.

If I learned the importance of smooth legs from young women's magazines, I also picked up suggestions concerning books to read that have stayed with me until this day. In the sixties and seventies, both *Seventeen* and *Mademoiselle* published short fiction and poetry. Both recommended literature in columns geared toward educating the tastes of a new generation of sophisticated young women. *Look Homeward, Angel* was one of the books. Thomas Wolfe's classic novel enthralled me in a way no literary work had yet done. The charming alcoholic father, the bossy, materialistic mother, and poor, misunderstood Eugene Gant— these people lived in my Lithuanian neighborhood.

I went on to read Wolfe's *Of Time and the River*. Like Eugene, I wanted to escape my provincial home town and run away to New York City. I began to write poetry:

> Time, time, time,
> What has become of mine?
> Has it all gone down to waste?
> In my hurry and my haste?

This very moment will never be.
It is lost in eternity.

The poem goes on for some time in this manner, ending in a couplet that advises the following strategy for existential angst:

The best that we can do each day,
Is to live our life in the fullest way.

I had enough confidence in my abilities as a poet to want to share the poem with others. Rita was not to be trusted; in a fit of envy she might claim the poem as her own. The few friends I had didn't care about important artistic endeavors. My parents were out of the question; they would ask me to write a poem in Lithuanian. This left Arvid, who had expanded his repertoire of buck-toothed expletives and had started calling me Buck-Buck, after a children's movie where a dog named Buck-Buck dies a sorrowful and unexpected death. "Please don' daah, Buck-Buck. Puh-leaz don' daah," the young Southern hero cries in the movie. "Please don' daah, Buck-Buck," Arvid groaned whenever I left the house.

Although I was bothered by Arvid's endless teasing about my teeth, out of all my classmates he had the most insight into poetry; classroom discussions revealed his understanding of the importance of rhyming. Besides, a relative had been a famous poet in Lithuania.

I invited him over for chamomile tea. I read my poem aloud as he helped himself to a slice of apple cake from the refrigerator.

"Daiva, this is good," he said. "Really really good."

I began to show him other poems. He showed me pictures he'd drawn of our seventh-grade teacher—a thin, bony, high-strung woman with the unfortunate name of Sister Marionette. He took complete advantage of her luckless moniker, depicting a puppetlike nun—*a marionette, get it*—with sticklike arms bent at ninety degree angles and toothpick legs extending in opposite directions.

Despite differences in temperament and intellectual development— "It's natural that girls mature more quickly than boys, Arvid," I told him—we both loved poetry and long philosophical discussions about time.

In addition, we shared a deeply felt patriotism toward Lithuania. We talked about going to live there; we imagined the rolling green hills and sparkling lakes we'd discover, the charming country cottages where storks nested atop shingled roofs, bringing luck to the homes' inhabitants. Unless of course we found a country where the grass glistened red from the blood of our countrymen, where people never smiled, where one's every movement was monitored by the telescopic eyes of the KGB. If the latter were the case, we'd start a revolution, kick the Communists reeling out of Lithuania.

While I read Lithuanian poetry and got good grades in Lithuanian Saturday School, Arvid actively recruited soldiers for his future liberation army. He had us write letters to President Nixon demanding sterner measures against the Soviet Union. He called for a boycott of Russian goods. He wrote and directed plays with Lithuanian themes and dreamed of performing them in front of large crowds unacquainted with our country's dire situation.

In the little white book labeled "8th Grade Autographs," the only entry written in Lithuanian is Arvid's. His handwriting is a series of childish flourishes striving for order: "I know that one day you'll be the world's greatest poetess. You will be known throughout the world and I am certain that you will win the Nobel Peace Prize. Stay true to your country and always labor so that she'll be free. Never forget me."

When Arvid's parents sent him to Fenwick High School, the then all-boys school run with military precision by the Dominicans, I thought I'd see much less of him and was surprised when he asked me to his homecoming dance. There was little sexual chemistry between us—I preferred boys with a spark of danger and a touch of aloofness while Arvid liked girls with straight teeth. But perhaps it was this lack of physical attraction that allowed us to have as much fun as we did. We danced the faster songs with abandon, furiously gyrating to "Twist and Shout." We sang along to "American Pie" and "The Candy Man." After the dance his brother picked us up. We went to Burger King and ate Whoppers and drank milkshakes until a fight broke out between two rival Mexican gangs and we all had to run for cover.

We spent New Year's Eve together that first year of high school. Arvid had set up a smorgasbord in his kitchen: piles of fried chicken, bread, potato and macaroni salads, banana cake, chocolate-covered cherries, Coke, and eggnog laced with rum. We played Scrabble—I beat him soundly, my diary entry reveals—and listened to tapes of Cheech and Chong.

My diary also states that we stayed up for hours after midnight walking the "dark, lonesome alleys" of Cicero, talking about God: "Is God a certain sex? Does it matter to him whether we pray on our knees or in bed? Does it matter whether we pray at all? Is there a heaven? Is there a God?"

I remained Arvid's next-door neighbor for at least eight more years. Although we attended the same commuter university, we rarely ran into each other. He was studying chemistry while I wavered between English and psychology. He had a steady girlfriend, a beautiful Jewish girl with hair down to her waist; I played the field with reckless abandon. I wouldn't see him for weeks when he'd show up at the door out of the blue and ask if I wouldn't mind calling him every morning at eight. The three alarm clocks he'd set at ten-minute intervals didn't always do the job; "I need a real live voice," he said.

"What if you don't hear the phone ringing?" I asked.

"Keep calling until I answer."

"If you didn't stay up until four in the morning, you wouldn't need three alarm clocks *and* a wake-up call."

"Just do it, Buck. Okay?"

We met for coffee sometimes. Once we drove to Union Pier, Michigan, to go to the beach. We waded along the shores of the lake, talking about the day we became neighbors.

"You called me an overgrown chick," Arvid said.

"You threw rocks at my window."

"Those were candies," he claimed.

"And the incident with the hotdog?"

"A highly revealing figment of your imagination."

At this reimagining of the past, I jumped into the water and began to dog-paddle away from the shore.

"You're too far out," Arvid yelled and leaped in after me.

I continued swimming, then suddenly stopped. I began to flail my hands, bobbing up and down as I yelled "help, help!" Arvid swam toward me with furious strokes. When he was a few feet away, I stood up on the sandbar, my hands clenched over my head like a boxer who'd just won a major fight.

We argued over religion. The questions we'd brought up that one New Year's Eve resurfaced, this time more eloquently stated. Arvid talked not only about God, but also about human responsibility for suffering and the complexity of salvation. I didn't want to talk about suffering. And salvation, as far as I was concerned, was found in a chilled bottle of white wine.

Increasingly, he talked about becoming a priest.

"Does your girlfriend know about this?" I asked him.

"I'm keeping it secret for now. Don't say anything, okay?"

"I want to marry you and Marty," Arvid tells me over the deep-dish pizza I have ordered for dinner.

"I don't think the Church allows polygamy."

"Don't be difficult, Buck."

"What's difficult will be getting the annulment."

"Not really. You weren't in your right mind when you married the first time," he assures me. "You were deluded and probably drunk."

"I don't even know if I believe in God."

"Marriage within the Church as opposed to living in sin might very well save you from eternal damnation."

"Fuck you, Arvid."

"No one's ever said fuck you to me," he admonishes.

"Not to your face," I mumble.

"Anyway, it should be 'Fuck you, *Father Arvid.*'"

He helps himself to another slice of pizza.

"Besides, a church wedding will make your mother happy."

Demonstrators on Cicero Avenue. Courtesy of Corbis Images.

Cicero

When I was in second grade, my father borrowed money from his bachelor friend Juozas Senkus for a down payment on a rickety wooden house. He rented the upstairs to *a nice couple*, who later turned out to belong to the Hell's Angels. The neighborhood was a step down in some ways, rougher, with fewer brick buildings and many more taverns. But the sense of Lithuanian community was stronger; St. Anthony's School with its adjacent church, a red brick Baroque-style building erected in 1906, had attracted a number of small businesses. Mr. Putrimas, the butcher, would slice the ham according to my mother's specifications and sometimes throw in a bone for the dog. A little further west, Mr. Stangenbergas and his wife owned a store, modest in size, darker, more enticing because of its wide selection of candy—not only Tootsie Rolls and Jujubes and Milk Duds, but strings of red licorice and huge, brightly colored jaw breakers and, best of all, big red wax lips that fit over our own. When we got tired of wearing the glamorous lips, we'd suck the sticky red sweetness out until all that was left was a big whitish ball of wax. (My sister and I were careful never to bring these home—confiscation of suspicious-looking candy, of which red wax lips topped the list, was an ever-present danger.)

We distrusted Mr. Stangenbergas with his shiny bald head, as round as a jawbreaker, his reserved manner, his strange name, a name that tripped on our tongues, a German-sounding name, and Germans, we had learned both at school and from our parents, were evil people. Not as evil as the Russians, but pretty darn close. The neighborhood children called him Hitler.

"Let's go to Hitler's," you'd hear at recess or lunchtime.

"We're going to Hitler's," my sister and I would announce after collecting our weekly allowance.

"I told you not to call him that," my mother would say, and explain to us again that Ponas Stangenbergas had come from the coastal city of Klaipėda, which once had belonged to Germany. She would make us repeat his name out loud, syllable by syllable—Stan-gen-ber-gas, Stan-gen-ber-gas.

"Okay, mom," I would say. "We're going to Stangenbergas's."

"Yeah, we're going to Hitler's," Rita would add and dash out of the house.

A few doors down from Hitler's, Dr. Kisielius ministered to a steady stream of patients in a small plain building whose only change over the forty years of its existence was the addition of iron bar windows sometime in the seventies. You didn't need an appointment to see Dr. Kisielius. You just showed up. If the waiting room was full you came back after an hour. He charged what patients could afford; he seemed to know when someone was out of a job. We rarely made fun of his name—*kisielius*—the rich cranberry pudding served only on Christmas Eve.

Across the street from Hitler's and Dr. Kisielius's, the Petkus Funeral Home stood as a constant reminder of life's inevitable conclusion. It was one of three funeral parlors on the block, all owned by second-

or third-generation Lithuanians. Death Row, some clever *lugan* had named the street. My classmate Gina Endriukaitis lived on Death Row, next door to Vance. A pretty and popular girl, she seemed completely oblivious to her unfortunate residence. I had a hard time just walking down the street, avoiding it whenever possible, yet here she was, yards away from dead bodies who might—*who knows*—rise up like zombies to stalk the nearby living.

Of the three funeral homes, Petkus was the most conveniently situated, kitty-corner from St. Anthony's; a body waked at Petkus could be easily transported to the church for the funeral mass the next morning. The pallbearers carrying the coffin, followed by a procession of relatives, friends, and neighbors, would move across the street as slowly as ships, stopping traffic for five minutes, or ten minutes, or even twenty, depending on the popularity of the recently deceased, as the magnificent church bell tolled.

That we lived so near the school conferred upon my sister and me the unearned but highly pleasurable status associated with location. We could walk home for lunch. We could walk to the drugstore, the source of my growing collection of comic books—everything from Richie Rich to Archie to Classic Comic Book renditions of Shakespeare. I read and reread them and stored them neatly in a large brown cardboard box I kept in the closet of the bedroom I shared with Rita. I counted the comics each night to make sure none had mysteriously disappeared.

I had friends, three in all. Across-the-Street-Diane wore orthopedic shoes and braces and was thus on the same disappointing page of pre-adolescent popularity as I was. Across-the-Alley-Diane, a year ahead of me in school, wore lip gloss and read *Tiger Beat* and possessed a glamour I could only dream about. With Antoinette (Tony) Zajauskas I shared a love of horses. We picked names for our imaginary equines with the same care other girls chose names for future babies: Flame, Silver Girl, Stormy Night. Neither of us had ever ridden on a horse, and we towered over our classmates, male and female, by half a foot, but that didn't stop us from eagerly anticipating future careers as jockeys.

We often played in the coal yard at the end of the block, my friends and I and sometimes Rita, friend-by-default, trying to capture rats until the owners confiscated our primitive cardboard traps. We moved onto bigger, easier prey, the cats that roamed the alley and were in great need of having their souls saved from the flames of eternal feline hell. We attempted to dress them up in makeshift white baptismal gowns constructed from pillow cases filched from the linen closet. In order to get the cats to relax, we resorted to the technique favored by grade-school children around the world—hypnotism. One of the Dianes would prop up an anxious tabby while Rita swung a pendant back and forth, back and forth. "You are now getting sleeeepy," she'd say. "Very very sleeepy." The cats never got sleepy. The drip drip drip of holy water—stolen from the fount at the entrance of our church—infuriated them. They scrambled from our arms, leaving us with scratches we later told classmates were stigmata.

We played along the train tracks, moving back only slightly when freight trains rumbled by. We yelled for chalk, jagged chunks of whitish limestone that the conductor sometimes tossed our way. We played in the alleys. *Mother, may I take two steps?* We searched the neighborhood garbage for valuables: a *Playboy* magazine, Miss October on the yellowing cover; a red-and-white polka-dotted shower cap; little squares of glass from the remnants of an altar discarded by the church—gold-flecked and sunflower yellow and a color I knew could only be cerulean.

Once I opened the lid of our own garbage to find the biggest treasure of all—a snake, inky black, silent and still at first, then thrashing its tail against the side of the can in a movement that both thrilled and terrified me. I yelled in my mangled, anglicized Lithuanian, "A snake has come to visit us!" My mother walked out with her broom, tipped the garbage can over on its side, then gently tapped the bottom as if she were loosening freshly baked muffins out of a pan.

During these years, my prized possession was a turquoise-blue Schwinn bike. It didn't have a banana seat, which my mother had deemed vulgar, and rust had begun to make its home on the back-wheel spokes, but I was as proud of that bike as a wealthy young playboy of his first Ferrari. Afternoons I would take off with great speed, pedaling as fast as I could away from home, eyeing landmarks to find my way back. To the south, the yellow brick house that once belonged to Al Capone stood out among the brownstones on the street like a platinum blonde in a room of brunettes. The house took up two lots, a luxury denied the other, plainer, buildings.

To the west the Barrett Varnish Company, a perfect upright domino of a structure, provided a point of reference. Past the varnish factory the streets stretched out for several miles, streets progressively cleaner, with fewer taverns and more brick buildings the closer one got to Berwyn. And more banks—the thrifty Czechs were famous for their flaky kolacky and their savings and loans. Berwyn came to a stop at the Cermak Plaza, a strip mall with a Woolworth's and a Tom McAn Shoes and a William A. Lewis; "Where the models buy their clothes" the sign outside the store announced.

The Eisenhower Expressway to the north provided another kind of boundary. I could cross the bridge to the other side, but the cars zooming by below made me nervous. What if I lost my balance? I imagined myself lurching past the railing down into the abyss of oncoming traffic.

The most dangerous barrier of all, however, was Cicero Avenue. Years later as a moody, rebellious teenager, I'd walk down Cicero, entranced by the life before me, the Mafia bars and strip joints and cheap motels. Men in beat-up Chevelles would sometimes yell, "Need a ride, hon?" I'd be relieved they never asked "How much?" as they did the women in red satin hot pants and halter tops and platform shoes who danced to some imaginary music on the corner of Cicero and Roosevelt.

As a child, however, I avoided Cicero Avenue because black people lived on the other side—the Chicago side—and black people, I'd been told by neighbors and friends of my parents, liked to steal the bikes of good but stupid white children who foolishly wandered into their territory. The reason that black people liked to steal bikes was because black people were different, not only in color but in attitude and upbringing. On the few occasions my mother took us downtown to buy the rare new dress at Goldblatt's, the neighborhoods we passed on the L didn't seem all that different from our own. There were grocery stores and taverns and churches. Children played kickball in the alleys; adults sat on stoops, smoking cigarettes. When the train curved slowly around a bend, I could peek into a building and see a woman ironing, or geraniums on a dusty windowsill, faded lace curtains fluttering in the breeze.

::::::::::::::

July 1966. Words dangle in the hot and heavy air, mingling with the smell of varnish and tobacco: *It's that King, King is behind it. That King that King that King.* "Who is that King?" I wonder, but not for long. My goals for the month consist of reading *Misty of Chincoteague* and ordering my secret decoder ring; the news that black people are going to march into my neighborhood and that white people do not want them to is just another unnecessary adult intrusion into the sacred geography of childhood.

As the summer wears on, however, *That King* takes on a more sinister note. I am told not to ride my bike anywhere near Cicero Avenue. My curfew is pushed back an hour. I observe the faces of my parents as they watch the ten o'clock news on their new black-and-white television. My usual mangling of the Zenith slogan—*The quality goes out when the name goes on*—fails to get a laugh. We spend a week in August at Eagle Lake, fishing for perch and bluegills during the day, playing Monopoly at night. It's only a temporary reprieve.

I can gauge the different reactions of the Lithuanians in the neighborhood toward the march by the suffixes they append to *juodas*, the word for black. The diminutive *ukas* ending results in *juodukas*, a harmless, sympathetic person, a *vargšelis*, a poor schmuck like the rest of us. *Juodis*, with its more formal *-is*, suggests an individual whom one dismisses with disapproval if not outright hostility. For the most part, my parents, especially my father, are *juodukas* people.

"I don't see how a black family living upstairs could be any worse than a tribe of Hell's Angels," he mumbles in Lithuanian between bites of cabbage.

"You're forgetting property values, Adolfai," my mother responds.

By the end of August even the neighborhood children are talking about the march. The older boy who lives a block away and goes to Roosevelt School and once showed me his penis, an absurd and ugly worm only slightly bigger than one of the night crawlers my father uses for fishing, asks me what I think about *that nigger King.*

"My parents told me not to say *nigger.* That's a bad word."

"Your parents are jag-offs."

"What's a jag-off?"

He shakes his head in disgust.

All the talk about *That King* makes me curious to see the man. That evening over dinner I ask my parents whether I can go to the march.

"Are you crazy?" my father yells. "What do you think this is going to be? A parade with floats and marching bands?"

We remain inside that Sunday afternoon, we Lithuanian kids, occasionally looking out the window hoping to catch a glimpse of some unfolding drama that will reassure us that where we live is worthy of television coverage. "Cicero is big, *vaikeli,*" my father says, "over six square miles." Resentful of his adult geography, the way he dampens my growing expectations with *vaikelis,* the diminutive of child, I sit in disappointed silence.

My nine-year-old conscience just barely registered the 2,700 National Guardsmen that lined the streets of the southern part of the city, the Cicero man killed by police, the over two hundred African Americans shoved back into their neighborhoods by a mob wielding rocks and bottles. I had more important things on my mind. School had started, and the joy of new notebooks and bright yellow No. 2 pencils and maybe even a pink plastic pencil-holder with multicolored psychedelic swirls displaced any thoughts of racial injustice.

In religion class we discussed the exact location of heaven. If heaven was "above"—and it said so in the hymns we sang—surrounding the earth like an extra stratosphere, then where, where was God? Spread around like a stick of butter on a particularly large and round and crusty bread roll? Where did all of those salvaged souls abide?

In biology we talked about evolution, which seemed to suck up every minute of science classes for years to come. I got the sense that the nuns would have just preferred that we sidestep the whole issue altogether, not because they didn't accept the notion that humankind had descended from lower forms of life—the Church had acknowledged the validity of evolution decades before—but because they were unable to answer our questions as to when it was, exactly, that man became man, that is, acquired a soul. Did Neanderthals have souls? we questioned. How about Cro-Magnon man?

"How about really really smart monkeys?" Arvydas Žygas had the nerve to ask.

Geography engendered much amusement. What could be funnier to a fourth grader than the name Lake Titicaca? Unless it was a photograph of yodelers in lederhosen. Other images, oddly poetic, piqued my interest: French villagers riding their bicycles through the countryside with long loaves of bread sticking out of backpacks like bleached baseball bats, Tokyo at night.

No one brought up race relations or questions of equality. Civics was always about populations, temperatures, and dates. In eighth grade a nun we all disliked dismissed the civil rights movement as so much hysteria. Once, when we were in the middle of whatever it was we were talking about, she told us to "quit acting like niggers." The class went absolutely still. We looked at each other in a kind of stilted silence; a few of us broke into laughter.

When it came time to choose a high school, my parents decided to send me not to all-girls Immaculate Heart of Mary, but to public Morton East. Money was tight, my parents told me, but I suspect they just got tired of all the questions about evolution.

My new classmates were mostly of Czech and Polish descent—Novaks and Cernys were as common as Smiths, and -inskis and -owskis filled up the rosters. Lithuanians and Italians were the minorities.

Despite my outward similarity to my classmates I felt like an outsider—I was shy and lumbering. My salvation was an introductory theater arts course I took as an elective. When our teacher, Miss Anderson, an unimposing woman with flat dark hair and glasses, asked us to interpret a poem as our first assignment, I chose Edna St. Vincent Millay's "Childhood Is the Kingdom Where Nobody Dies." My effort was greeted with a word I had seldom heard from the reticent nuns— "excellent." The Lithuanian tradition of poetry recitation had prepared me for my first foray into oral interpretation in English. I knew that poems were meant to be read out loud. I recognized the importance of eye contact, of subtle gesture. I understood that pauses came at the end of sentences, not at the conclusion of lines.

My sophomore year I got the lead in *Cactus Flower*, the role of Stephanie, the nurse, played by Ingrid Bergman in the movie. It was a coup for me. The applause, the review in the school paper—all this created a surge of confidence that carried over to other aspects of my life. Most gratifying was the respect from my peers, the outsiders who peopled the theater classes, who sewed the costumes and built the sets, who listened to Dylan and sometimes smoked pot in Billy Lee's basement.

My junior year I received a letter from a man named Floyd Seahorn. He'd seen a photograph of me in the *Cicero Life* advertising our high school production of *Barefoot in the Park*:

> Dear Daiva,
>
> I know that most white people in Cicero doesn't like black people. And I thought maybe you feel the same way. Do you, Daiva? I hope not. . . . If you hate black people what is your reason for doing so?
>
> Most young white people hate black people because this is something the old people has put in their minds. I don't think another person should tell anyone who to love and not love. God said to love everyone. And to me, that's the first and last word.
>
> Let me tell you a few things about myself. As you can see by the number behind my name on the envelope, I'm in jail. Please don't judge me as no-good because I'm in jail. I didn't come here for hurting anyone.
>
> I am 23 years old, 5'10," 150 pounds, brown eyes, black hair, and

*complexion is dark brown. My home is Chicago. I am doing 3 years for
having $75,000 in Counterfeit Money. I got about 18 more months to go.*

    *If you send me a picture of you, it'll make me very happy. Will you
please send me one of your beautiful pictures?*

    *Please don't think I'm saying you're one of those peoples that hate all
black people. You don't look to be that kind of young lady.*

    *Well, that's all I have to say, and I wish you send me the picture, and
also I hope you and I can become the best of friends.*

    Love and peace,

    Floyd

    My mother managed to confiscate the letter and quickly nixed my dreams of a passionate, revolutionary correspondence.

In college I began to lie about Cicero, denying it as my birthplace, my childhood neighborhood, my home. The university, an L ride away, had increased my exposure to liberal politics. I took a class with Dick Simpson, the maverick alderman who was a perpetual thorn in the side of the Daleys. I studied theater and got a part as a chorus member in *Oedipus.*

    "Where are you from?" cast members asked.

    "I was born at the place where three roads meet," I'd answer.

    Or: "I come from the land of ice and snow."

    Or sometimes: "I live in the western suburbs."

    "*Which* western suburb?"

    "Berwyn."

    I often set foot in Berwyn. I *could* have lived in Berwyn.

    When the well-off suburban parents of a man I was in love with and later considered marrying asked where I lived, I couldn't lie. "Cicero," I said. "I'm from Cicero." I paused, then added: "Cicero. Like the great Roman orator."

    They looked at their beautiful, brilliant son, a conscientious objector, and then they looked at me as if I were the kind of woman who wrote fan letters to Richard Nixon.

    A tiny rage welled up inside, a feeling that frightened me with its potential. Their house, a single-family residence with two bathrooms and a fireplace and a finished basement would have been a mansion in Cicero. A black BMW sat in the garage, a bottle of Joy on the bathroom counter. There were no black people in the neighborhood except for the ladies who came twice a week to clean the big houses and the men who took away the garbage.

I sometimes go back to visit Cicero, usually to take my mother to Sunday Mass at St. Anthony's. She is hoping that Father Trimakas, the Lithuanian priest, will help spread the word to God that at eighty-three she is not yet ready to let the cancer whittling away at her body carve her up completely. She has things to do, people to visit, letters to write, books to read. The English-speaking God that presides at St. Germaine's, the church within walking distance of her condominium in Oak Lawn, may not have gotten the message.

The Lithuanian service has been moved to nine in the morning. The Mexicans have garnered the popular eleven o'clock slot, amid flurries of protest from the Lithuanians, of whom there are fewer, but who have been there, as they will quickly point out, much longer.

Today my mother is restless. She looks around the church, fixing her gaze on the statue of St. Anthony holding the Christ Child. She waves occasionally to an old familiar friend. "Let us fall to our knees, all of us Christians," she joins in singing—"Pulkim ant kelių, visi krikščionys"— though she can barely stand, let alone kneel.

After the service we walk around the block, my mother clutching my arm.

"The houses, they've gotten smaller," I tell her.

"And more frail," she adds in Lithuanian.

They are much less sturdy than the inhabitants themselves, some of whom are sitting on the front steps of porches or driving around the block in big old cars of indeterminate makes and models. The sidewalks appear to have shrunk. The children playing hopscotch aren't aware of this incredible disappearing concrete. A little Mexican boy rides his bicycle as if it were a truck and he the driver on his own personal highway—I think of my Schwinn.

It comes back to me how much I loved this neighborhood, a place that by all accounts I should have loathed, the City of Brotherly Hate, the Selma of the North. A manufacturing town, its primary industry dampers and shutters, an ugly place stinking of whiskey and cabbage, a Nowhere-land of corrupt politicians and gangsters.

What lingers in memory, however, is the church bell of St. Anthony's, its chime superior to that of St. Attracta's, the Italian parish three blocks north. What else remains: the cats that roamed the alleys, the bookmobile glinting in the afternoon sun, the aroma of Atomic Fireballs when the wind blew from the Ferrara Pan Candy Company to the west. And the snake, its head a black leather bullet, its body an omen of beautiful and dangerous things to come.

"Do you remember the big black snake?" I ask my mother.

"What are you talking about?"

"In the garbage can."

How does she not remember the big black snake?

"It was probably a garden hose," she says.

A *mercado* across the street from the church sells milk and bread and apricot nectar, and also jawbreakers and Jujubes, though I can't find the big red wax lips and don't know how to ask for them in Spanish.

"The salesman, he doesn't speak a word of English," my mother whispers. "Can you believe it?"

As we walk back to the car, we hear in the near distance a vaguely familiar tune played in double time on a rowdy accordion. It reminds me of the polkas we practiced at Lithuanian Saturday School at the end of the regular lessons, a reward for the correct conjugation of verbs. My mother's eyes light up. I think she's going to start dancing: step step step hop, step step step hop. I don't have the heart to tell her the song isn't even Lithuanian, but a Mexican *norteño* from south of the Rio Grande. Its melody suggests a life beyond the workaday world of factories and repair shops and taco stands, the sweetly remembered existence of another country, another life.

With my sister (*right*) and cousin Andy

Waiting Tables

The summer I was eighteen I worked as a waitress at Tabor Farm, a golf resort in southwest Michigan. From the talent shows the staff put on every Sunday in the old barn to the apple pie the guests ordered for dessert, Tabor Farm exuded an almost exaggerated wholesomeness. "Tabor Farm: Family Resort" a carved wooden sign in the lobby read, lest anyone mistake it for something else—say, a nudist colony. The only detail out of place in this Norman Rockwell picture of American vacation happiness was that the owner, Valdas Adamkus, had fled Lithuania during the Second World War, eventually settling in Hinsdale, Illinois; out of the staff of waitresses, busboys, and cook's helpers, about half were the sons and daughters of Lithuanian immigrants like himself. My friends Daina and Natalija worked there, as did Arvid, my next-door neighbor in Cicero, Illinois. We were happy to have these glamorous jobs. While our non-Lithuanian friends were miserably flipping burgers at minimum wage, we were fetching martinis and learning important French phrases such as *coq au vin* and *au jus*.

During the week, Mr. Adams, as the customers called him, worked in Chicago for the Environmental Protection Agency; his wife Alma ran Tabor Farm. She oversaw the menus, ordered the food, made sure that the customers were satisfied and that the young Lithuanian help, especially the girls, stayed out of serious trouble. She feared that we would drown in the pool or, worse, run off with the locals, boys with names like Chuck and Randy, who were clearly not college bound. What would she tell our parents? She was a slim, elegant, somewhat shy woman who was prone to allergies and headaches. Every Friday morning she drove into Benton Harbor to get her light blonde hair coiffed. Friday evenings Valdas would arrive for the weekend, and a newfound energy would infuse her being.

They were a handsome couple, devoted to each other in the openly affectionate way that older childless couples sometimes are. Mr. Adams spoke English like our fathers did—"You vahnt mohr gravy?" he would ask, assisting behind the buffet table at lunch. Unlike our fathers, however, he never raised his voice. A single glance was enough to instill respect. Once, when Daina and her boyfriend Romas wandered down to the melon patch in the stealth of the night and crept back with armloads of contraband cantaloupes, he was there, standing against the barn, a shadowy figure in the darkness. "He didn't say a word," Daina told me later. "I couldn't face him for weeks."

We were friendly, hardworking kids. We got along with the difficult adults there: Joe, the cook, who claimed to have worked for Elizabeth Taylor and who, we suspected, drank in secret. And Martha, who confused our names, not because she was going senile, but because she was going deaf. She was a Midwestern version of Granny from *The Beverly Hillbillies*: short, stubborn, wearing her big shoes and her hairnet with as much panache as if they were glamorous Hollywood accessories. She had been a career waitress of sorts, and felt that standards had dipped dangerously low. Her constant concern was that the sugar bowls on each table were not being refilled on a regular basis. Her refrain—"Sugar bowls, girls! Sugar bowls!"—echoed throughout the dining room long after dinner was over. She had no family that we knew of. She lived for waitressing and the Detroit Tigers, whose games she listened to on an old transistor radio glued to her ear.

The waitresses lived in a long narrow concrete building that had once housed chickens while the boys had their own lodgings a safe and respectable distance away. The rooms were small and dark, but they were ours. We taped posters to the walls—the Moody Blues, Bob Dylan, the Who; they unfurled in the summer heat. We tried to keep plants; they withered due to lack of indoor light. We burned incense and walked barefoot to the pool on our days off. We lived for these days, and for Saturday mornings, when the customers we had waited on for the entire week would calculate how much our services were worth and stuff their decisions in plain white envelopes with our names, often misspelled—Diava, Dina, Natalya—scrawled on the top.

Like other activities that entailed a certain sense of coordination and grace, waitressing did not come easily to me. I was nervous, too eager to please, and this anxiety caused me to confuse orders, to slam food down on the table, to stutter my apologies. Once, when I finally thought I was getting the hang of things and was proudly balancing a plate of Hawaiian ham in one hand and two side dishes of carrots in the other, I watched in horror as the pineapple slice atop the ham took on a life of its own and slid off its plate onto the lap of a white-pantsuit-clad dentist's wife from Waukegan.

That my busboy was frequently Arvid made matters worse—we had a history as complicated as the Middle East's. For years we'd hurled invectives across the fence: *Hey Buck! Hey Raisin-head!* There followed an era when Arvid would visit almost every day, ignoring me completely, but helping himself without restraint to food in our refrigerator, a habit my mother did nothing to discourage. "The son I never had," she sometimes called him. He praised her leftover meatloaf, her choice of fruit juices, her Jell-O molds, with bits of grapes and strawberries floating in them, he said, "like lost matter in the cosmos."

In the last year or so we had shifted to a more mature manner of communicating. Sometimes Arvid would come over after school and we'd sip herbal tea with honey and listen to Leonard Cohen, singing along to "Famous Blue Raincoat."

At Tabor Farm, however, we reverted to our worst, most childish, behavior.

"Table 8 wants to speak to you," I'd say during dinner.

"What about?"

"Your substandard service."

Arvid would rush up and begin to apologize, only to be met with uncomprehending stares.

Sometimes, however, my busboy was tall, sanguine Geoff, or better yet, his best friend—dark-haired, dimpled David. Both were college students, which made them instantly desirable. Geoff was an art major at Ball State University. He made fun of Ball State—*My God, what a name*. David, too, found a way to transform the simplest of words, inflecting every little phrase with delectable nuance. He gave me books to read, Günter Grass's *The Tin Drum*, Márquez's *A Hundred Years of Solitude*, inscribing the inside cover of the latter with "Just something for being so nice. Read and enjoy. . . . Love, David S."

I pondered these simple words—"Love, David S."—as if repeated readings would reveal some deeper meaning I had missed the first time. I began to wear cologne—Je Reviens. *I will return.* I couldn't understand why Daina and Natalija had boyfriends, serious boyfriends who bought them heart-shaped gold-plated pendants and took them to the movies, whereas my experiences with the opposite sex had been limited to peripheral flirtations, occasional drunken gropings in the back seats of cars, and crushes on boys like David, who finally admitted to me that he'd never had a real girlfriend, and didn't think he ever would.

I began to wonder whether there was a connection between my lack of confidence in waitressing and my disappointing experiences with men. Perhaps the trick with both, as with so many other things in life, was to relax, to try and attain a state of Zen-like acceptance. I practiced deep breathing before lunch. I muttered "om" under my breath. I engaged in mental word play, pondering the meanings and possible origins of certain phrases while I waited for my orders to come in. *Hole-in-one*, for example. If a particularly talented and lucky golfer made several of these, would that make them *holes-in-one*, or *hole-in-ones*? And wouldn't the more precise term really be *ball-in-one*, I mustered up the courage to ask a few baffled customers. I reflected on the absurdity of *waiting tables*, a term that brought to mind lonely kitchen furniture hoping for human companionship. *Waiting on tables* conjured up even more ridiculous images—slovenly waitresses sprawled across dining room tables as families wandered in for lunch.

It was at this pivotal point in my waitressing career that I met him—Robert Miller, or at least that's what I think his name was. He was there with his daughter, a slender girl of eleven or twelve with hair down to her waist. Robert Miller was beautiful as well, a tall man whose thick blond hair had begun to fade into ashy grayness. He dressed up for dinner in tan cotton slacks and shirts I was sure could only come from Brooks Brothers. He had the same shy smile as his daughter. In a dining room full of boisterous families and chatty retired couples, father and daughter stood out like two long-stemmed roses in a field of daisies.

"Do you golf?" he asked me that first day as I poured him coffee.

"What's the point of trying to force a small white ball into a small dark hole?" I answered.

He smiled.

I blushed.

The next evening he asked where I was planning to go to college—as if such a decision were left solely up to me. I was too embarrassed to tell him that it was going to be the large urban campus that Daina and Arvid were going to attend, where almost *all* the Lithuanian kids went.

"I want to be an actress," I told him. "A *professional* actress."

"I'm a lawyer. A professional lawyer."

"I imagine there must be similarities between the two careers," I said knowingly.

Robert Miller laughed.

He told me I reminded him of a painting by Renoir that hung in the Art Institute, a portrait of a child with blond hair and round apple cheeks. Did I know the painting he was referring to?

On the last day of his vacation Robert Miller asked if I'd want to take a walk after dinner. We strolled over to the apple orchards at the edge of the resort. As the warmth of the summer evening faded into a pleasant coolness and the smell of lilacs infused the air, he kissed me. It was neither a long nor a particularly passionate kiss, but in the moonlit field far from my little room it marked a passage from the world of boys who ignored my pathetic attentions to men who believed I was the kind of girl who frequented the Art Institute on a regular basis.

The weekend after Labor Day, Tabor Farm was transformed from a respectable family resort to the annual carnival of Lithuanian artists, academics, and self-described intellectuals calling themselves *santariečiai*. They had been coming to Tabor Farm since 1959, when a small group of college students merged with an older group formed in a Displaced Persons camp in Tübingen, Germany, the *šviesiečiai*, to form a progressive organization called Santara-Šviesa (Unity / Light). My mother and her brother had been founding members of the latter group. Perhaps the pastoral setting—the apple orchards, the river that bordered one side of the resort—reminded them of Lithuania. Perhaps the distance from Chicago, specifically, from Marquette Park Lithuanians with their reactionary politics, their prescriptive Catholicism, was a drawing point; here they could argue and drink in peace.

The differences between the two groups at Tabor Farm—the Americans throughout the summer, the Lithuanians that one long weekend in September—were obvious to any outsider after a day's observation. The American women wore shorts and Lacrosse tops in pastel colors; the men dressed for golf. You'd see the *santarietės* in loose black pants and tops, or dresses in exuberant African prints, the younger ones in Levi's and peasant blouses. Chunks of amber dangled from their necks. The men wore jeans or Sansabelt slacks; a few sported bell-bottoms, although these had gone out of style years ago. Whereas the Americans golfed and never got publicly drunk, the Lithuanians drank heavily, publicly, with great enthusiasm. They rarely, if ever, played golf.

Growing up, I had heard both about the drinking and the heady cultural atmosphere of Santara-Šviesa, heard about the stories of the more distinguished members, their difficult, important books, their complicated lives. They were geniuses, artistes, larger than life. Some had defected from Soviet-occupied Lithuania in the late 1960s amid rumors that had rocked the Lithuanian community. While most diaspora Lithuanians looked upon them as heroes, others believed they were spies, sent by the Communists to report on the goings-on of their noble, freedom-loving compatriots.

They may have been geniuses, but waiting on them was a pain in the ass. Some wandered in late for breakfast, bleary-eyed, nursing hangovers from the night before, demanding endless refills of coffee. By lunch they had switched to beer. Some of the older men pinched my behind and called me *mergaite*—girl.

At least one of the men was certifiably crazy, convinced that the beet salad was poisoned. He confessed to me that he had been locked up in a Soviet mental institution for his political beliefs and fed mind-altering drugs. "I know you won't tell anyone," he whispered. "Not a pretty girl like you."

Some, like Tomas Venclova, one of Lithuania's most famous poets and a highly respected literary critic, were enigmatic figures, strange as Dalí paintings. He rattled through his brilliant lectures and wore the same heavy black wool turtleneck sweater the whole weekend, though the early September sun was warm enough for swimming. I was his waitress one morning.

"How do you like your eggs?" I asked him in Lithuanian.

He didn't know what I meant. As I repeated the question, translating word for word in my broken Lithuanian, struggling to find the words for "sunny-side up" and "scrambled," I realized that I was asking him whether he liked his eggs "like balls." I looked around helplessly for someone to come to the rescue. But Venclova was by himself, as I would see him other times, other places, solitary, reluctant to join others in the daily ritual of small talk.

The women seemed as unusual as the men. There was the artist who went by a single name. Her eyes, lined heavily in black, seemed to turn up slightly at the edges, like her question mark of a smile. The women in her cartoonlike drawings resembled forest sprites on speed. One summer they lined the walls of the barn; their loopy oddness bespoke a generational difference in taste. The older *santariečiai*, even those who thought themselves thoroughly modern, looked confused.

There was the writer Eglė Juodvalkytė who, in a single stroke of linguistic derring-do, lopped the "ytė" from her surname, the suffix that announced to the world that she was a single woman, and became the androgynous Juodvalkė. "Neither here nor there," harrumphed some of the men, though I think they felt threatened. And the poet Liūnė Sutema, whose name, as strange and mysterious as her writing—*sutemti* means to darken—I loved to utter even after my mother told me it was a nom de plume.

In between waitressing, I attended the lectures and panel discussions that took place in the old barn. Mornings were often devoted to literature—talks on the problematic modernism of Antanas Škėma, on the death and rebirth of the avant-garde theater in Lithuania. The afternoon sessions, often of a political nature—underground movements in Soviet Lithuania, evolving ethnic consciousness among young Lithuanian-Americans—were the most heavily attended. The question-and-answer periods were spirited, sometimes contentious. Individuals who threatened to drone on with mini-lectures of their own were greeted with rising murmurs of "What's your point?"

Most animosities were wiped out after a night of heavy drinking. The *santariečiai* began their revels in the little bar off the lobby of the main building, downing vodka, that gift from the colonizers, or guzzling beer. They would continue their merry-making after closing time, some careening arm in arm to the banks of the St. Joseph's River, where someone might build a campfire (and someone else might stumble into the fire.) You'd hear them at 4 a.m. belting out *Išgerkim, broleli*—let's drink, my brother—as if what they'd been doing for the past eight hours was playing checkers.

I continued to attend Santara long after my waitressing career at Tabor Farm was finished, driving there with my parents, then separating from them as quickly as I could, sometimes heading straight to the bar for a vodka martini.

Czeslaw Milosz spoke at Santara one summer, several years before he was awarded the Nobel Prize. The reading room was packed. I half expected a thin dark-eyed figure with sloping shoulders—my idea of a poet—when Milosz appeared: a broad-shouldered man with a face as Lithuanian as a country ham. Milosz's mother had been born and raised in Žemaitija—Milosz had gone on to write about Lithuania in several of his books. The themes of exile and dislocation that are so often found in his poems resonated with this Lithuanian audience. That he spoke and wrote in Polish—was Polish—didn't matter to them, though his ethnicity would have been an issue to the lowest common denominator of Lithuanian, for whom a Pole was a dirty Pole, *better to have nothing to do with the devils.*

Joseph Brodsky read his poems at Santara. I didn't know who he was then, this man who looked like a paunchy James Caan. Later I bragged to friends how this great Russian poet—a Nobel Prize winner—had left his sophisticated New York City dwelling (for so I had imagined it) to spend a weekend at Tabor Farm: Family Resort.

At Santara I came into contact with individuals who fell outside of what I had internalized to be the traditional definition of Lithuanian: someone who was Catholic. Here were Lithuanian Lutherans, and Lithuanian agnostics and avowed atheists. Here were Lithuanian Jews. The dissident political analyst Alexandras Štromas, who had predicted the fall of the Soviet Union back at a time when this was unthinkable, was a Santara regular along with his much younger wife, Violeta, a petite, dark-haired cabaret singer. They made an interesting couple: Jabba the Hutt and Audrey Hepburn.

Icchokas Meras, a Lithuanian Jew who had escaped the Holocaust when an illiterate mother of six took him in and raised him as her own, read from his work at Santara. His novel *Striptizas* (Striptease) had been serialized in Communist Lithuania in the literary journal *Pergalė* (Victory). The authorities had found it subversive, its experimental form veering too far away from the tenets of Soviet literary realism, its extensive symbolism obviously attempting to convey a critique of the political system.

I spoke to Meras afterward.

"I write," I told him in Lithuanian. "I want to be a writer."

He smiled and nodded his head.

"Should I write in English or Lithuanian?"

I waited for him to tell me that I must write in Lithuanian, that if I didn't I would be responsible for the death of the oldest living European language.

"I get the sense that English comes more naturally to you," he said politely.

"Yes," I nodded.

"Then you must write in English."

For years I came and just listened, though I longed to ask questions: What role would women play in a newly reconstituted Lithuania? Is diaspora literature doomed to endless thematic repetition? I was afraid that the Lithuanian that had garnered me compliments in the émigré community-at-large might very well be greeted with scorn here in this rarified company of poets, journalists, linguists, politicians—masters of the language.

Looking back on this period of my life, I don't think I really wanted answers to these questions as much as I wanted to be seen as intelligent and sophisticated, a young woman to be reckoned with. I wanted to be like Ilona Maziliauskienė, who had a crowd hanging onto her every word when she talked about the modern Lithuanian novel. She was blunt, somewhat careless in her appearance, with a voice that suggested nights drinking whiskey and smoking cigarettes. I wanted to be like Violeta Kelertienė, who once told the Lithuanian men in the audience that "feminist" was not a dirty word. She told them that they were behind the times, and, in so many words, *excuse the expression, full of shit.*

Valdas Adamkus sold Tabor Farm in the early 1990s. Soon after, he ran for the presidency of Lithuania. He defeated his opponent by a narrow margin, the deciding votes cast by people like my mother, who lived in Chicago and visited Lithuania now and again. Those of us who worked for Adamkus at Tabor Farm were surprised at neither his election nor his successful tenancy. We knew that anybody who could effectively deal with teenagers would do just fine running a small country.

Shortly after Adamkus's election, Santara moved to the Lithuanian World Center in Lemont, a suburb of Chicago. Although it has lost some of its cultural cachet and much of its rowdy, drunken atmosphere, the annual gathering remains a popular venue for scholars and artists. A decade ago, the organizers asked me to read a chapter from my dissertation on the letter-writing habits of Lithuanian immigrants. My mother helped me translate the paper into Lithuanian. I practiced reading out loud—slowly, with appropriate pauses and a few spontaneous-sounding interjections.

"You have to really stretch that *eh* sound," my mother warned. "Remember, the *e* has a *nosinę*."

Although I was nervous, that day marked a turning point in my self-perception as an academic. I still struggle with Lithuanian, my mother tongue, my *mother's* tongue. When I dream, I dream in English. I curse in English. But I read Lithuanian poetry and follow Lithuanian politics. The art that hangs on my walls is by Lithuanian artists. Sometimes I even write in Lithuanian, slowly and carefully, attempting to gather the unruly black sheep that threaten any minute to rebel.

My mother's uncle and family in Siberia

The Lithuanian Dictionary of Depression

With each passing year my parents grew more accustomed to their life in America. They put money in high-yield savings accounts, supported the local Lithuanian Saturday School and the Cicero Public Library, subscribed to the Lithuanian daily *Draugas* and the Book of the Month Club, and voted in both national and local elections. Occasionally, however, they lapsed into reveries of sadness and concern; their melancholy was most palpable on days when letters arrived from Lithuania. For every four or five letters my parents sent relatives during those cold war years, they received one, admonishing them for not writing: *Dear Adolfai, we are doing well except for the inevitable sicknesses. We are lucky when we can get aspirin. Why don't you write? Please write. Perhaps you have forgotten us, what with your fancy cars and automatic washing machines.*

141

The first time I saw my father cry was when a letter arrived from Lithuania, on paper thin as skin, saying that his mother had died. Her already fragile lungs had collapsed under the strain of the Siberian winter. Her last breath froze in midair; that's how I pictured it in sixth grade. In her one existing photograph, black and white, her deeply lined unsmiling face, shrouded by a black babushka, bears witness to a grim existence—a difficult husband; one son, the beloved, killed in a mining accident in Vorkuta, his body sliced in half by a machine whose job it was to shatter large and stubborn chunks of coal; another son destroyed by vodka; yet another, my father, lost in that difficult hour when the desire to remain with his wife and newborn daughter in Dusetos was overpowered by a stark vision of life under the Russians. And then of course there was the deportation itself, the uprooting, the loss of the little farm, the garden she found solace in, planting tomatoes, tending to the rue. Their names had found their way onto Stalin's dreaded list— they were Enemies of the People because of an unregistered hunting rifle my grandfather had owned.

My mother's more privileged family had also boarded one-way trains for Siberia. Great-Aunt Irena, forewarned by a neighbor that a disgruntled servant had spoken to the authorities about some small, perhaps imaginary slight, buried the good family china in the middle of the night beneath the shadow of the largest oak. Fifty years later, after the restoration of independence, her children unearthed the delicate cups and saucers, the dishes encrusted with mud, but still whole, still usable. That same year they dug up the bones of their father and grandmother, brought them back from Siberia to the warmer soil of Suvalkija.

Sometimes, however, my parents' sadness had less to do with harsh political realities than with bittersweet remembrances of youth, often evoked by music or nature. Beethoven's Sixth Symphony, the *Pastoral*, provoked the same response in my father every time the flute emerged from the surrounding forest of strings in the second movement. "Listen to the cuckoo's call," he'd say. And then, in wonder, "You've never heard a cuckoo!" My sister and I would roll our eyes. "That's because there are no cuckoos in America, da-ad," I'd answer. A trip through the Wisconsin countryside would bring back memories of the forests of Lithuania with their birches and pines. My mother would speak of the holiness of trees, their sacred status in Lithuanian culture.

"The souls of the dead migrate to surrounding oaks and maples," she would explain as matter-of-factly as if she were telling us where birds go in the winter.

A stay at the Indiana Dunes would invite the inevitable comparison with Palanga. "After a storm, my brothers and I would run to the beach and gather bits of amber," my mother would reminisce. "Here, of course, there is no amber."

In general, the men in the family were more resilient than the women in dealing with the day-to-day concerns of life and the gusts of melancholy that arose like a strong and unexpected northerly wind. A fondness for routine coupled with a sure sense of their place in the Lithuanian patriarchal order prevented both my father and my grandfather—my mother's father—from slipping into extended bouts of sadness.

Accustomed to a life of hard physical labor as a boy, my father would begin his day with half an hour of jumping jacks and deep-knee bends from a booklet published by the U.S. Air Force Academy. After eating the eggs and toast prepared by my mother, he'd grab the thermos of coffee she'd hand him on the way out. He'd arrive early at the engineering firm where he worked for many years as a draftsman. He was a steady, reliable employee, careful not to let a weekend's worth of living it up interfere with Monday morning responsibilities.

On those evenings when my father wasn't at school completing his engineering degree, he'd sit in the living room puffing on a cigar and listen to records, vinyl LPs he didn't let my sister or me touch. His taste was eclectic; he enjoyed opera and Lithuanian folk songs and American country music. A Brahms string quartet might be followed by Hank Williams singing about "them ol' cotton fields back home." The Kingston Trio's rendition of Nancy Whiskey would tread on the heels of Mahler's *Das Lied von der Erde*.

My grandfather, my mother's father, also lived a life governed by self-imposed routines; by training he was a mathematician. He addressed my grandmother in the formal *jūs* instead of the intimate, expected *tu*. He was friendly, if not affectionate, toward his grandchildren, saving his energies for his daily mile-and-a-half walk and his two-hour perusal of both *Draugas* and its rival paper, *Naujienos*. My grandfather ate a raw onion every day, peeling back the layers slowly with a paring knife. He lived to be ninety-six.

Among his later-life passions was writing. Like many of his peers, my grandfather published his memoirs: *Sketches of the Past* he called the book, funded by his youngest brother, Kazys, a prosperous farmer who'd immigrated to Canada from Lithuania. The action in *Sketches* is recounted in the formal language of a man deeply uncomfortable with the vocabulary of feeling. There is no mention of my grandmother—their courtship and marriage—or of his children. Affection intrudes upon the narrative only once, when my grandfather writes about his grandfather, a beekeeper, who would bless his bees with the sign of the cross before attending to them. He once scolded his grandson for saying that some of the bees had *keeled over*: "You have to say that they died."

The fact that sentiment is largely absent from *Sketches of the Past* is not surprising. My grandfather had no patience for anything that interfered with his orderly, uncomplicated life. Once, when my mother was complaining about the rising cost of Catholic school tuition and my grandmother was grousing about the bad manners of the neighborhood children, my grandfather announced: "I have an idea. Why don't we go into the backyard, dig a really deep hole, and all jump in?"

Compared to my taciturn grandfather, my grandmother was a complainer of gold medal caliber. She found the small apartment in Cicero stifling, the opera too expensive, the women with curlers in their hair shouting at their children in the laundromat undignified. Even the workers, members of the so-called Democratic Party, seemed more loyal to Mayor Daley than to any principles of international brotherhood, so unlike the social democrats she had known and supported back in Lithuania.

Of the many indignities cast upon my grandmother in this new country, the greatest was English itself. She was in her sixties when she came to America, too old, she said, to learn another language. My grandmother rarely ventured outside. With her grandchildren growing older and her husband involved with his writing, she spent her days sleeping and eating and complaining and watching television in a language she claimed to despise.

"Do you think *močiutė* could have been clinically depressed?" I asked my mother once.

"Clinically?" she said and wrinkled her nose. "I don't know what that means."

We took the English-Lithuanian Dictionary off the shelf. There was no definition for "clinically" or "clinical."

"Your grandmother endured many losses," she continued. "Her mother at a young age. Her brother during Stalin's purges."

"Others lost entire families. Children, spouses, parents. Others still waved their flags at Vasario 16 meetings and baked *krustai* and wrote letters to *Draugas.*"

"You are being judgmental."

Like my grandmother, my mother was sensitive to slights, both real and perceived. She felt things deeply. She took Milltown for her migraines and valium for her nerves. I once came upon her sitting on the couch with her head in her hands, weeping, listening to the chorus of the Hebrew slaves from Verdi's *Nabucco* on the classical music station.

"What's wrong?" I asked her.

"Nothing," she said and looked up. "We are born, we suffer, we marry, we suffer, we bear children, we suffer, we grow old, and we die."

She was consumed by anxieties that threatened to fill the space around her like the carbon monoxide she feared might kill us all. She was frightened of driving a car and never got her license. I tried to teach her once—I'd been a late bloomer myself when it came to driving, and thought my patience and maturity would work to her advantage. After a shaky Sunday morning start, my mother's hands gripping the wheel as if holding on to a life preserver, we came to an intersection without a stop sign. It was clear that the cars on Austin Avenue, the bigger street, had the right of way. My mother, instead of slowing down before crossing, simply closed her eyes and continued.

"Mom, you *have* to keep your eyes open when you drive," I yelled. "That's a basic rule."

"Why do you always criticize me?" my mother asked.

Not only driving a car, but riding *in* a car produced anxiety in my mother. Her rules for living safely in the world included avoiding the front passenger seat as often as possible.

"Always sit in the back," she'd tell me.

"Why?"

"You're more likely to survive an accident."

"But what if I'm on a date?"

"Your date will understand."

She was the first mother in the neighborhood to learn the Heimlich maneuver. Even before this, she had her own methods of dealing with choking, garnered from her brother, a doctor, to whom she'd admitted that she had almost died chewing on a Lifesaver: "You need to scream as loud as you can. That loosens the vocal cords."

My mother's depression was mitigated by the hope she had for the future of her children as well as by a few simple things that gave her pleasure: British comedies on PBS, peach pie with vanilla ice cream, the household plants that thrived under her gentle, experienced care. She loved beautiful, more costly things as well. Our house was filled with paintings: several important Petravičiuses; two or three Ignas graphics; an expensive Domšaitis—an oil of a few small apples and a withering pear lounging in a blue ceramic bowl, a solitary lemon leaning against the bowl upon a wooden table.

"I feel like that lemon," my mother told me more than once.

Because the Lithuanian Dictionary of Depression contains only two entries—1) Grief Caused by War / Exile and 2) the Inevitable Sadness of Existence—I was stuck with a limited vocabulary when I experienced my first episode, during the summer of 1981. My life seemed to change overnight from mildly chaotic to disturbing, though in retrospect the signs had been pointing to a psychic breakdown for some time. The black dog, Winston Churchill called depression, and perhaps that image comes closest to evoking the nature of the beast. You turn around: the dog is always there, though sometimes he sits on his haunches and watches at a distance and sometimes he nips at your heels, trying to nudge you into a corner with silent determination.

One June evening, standing on the platform of the Dearborn L stop in downtown Chicago where I worked, I was transfixed by the electric spark of an oncoming train. "Jump," a voice whispered. I stepped back and closed my eyes and counted to twenty. Safely inside the train, I looked around to see a woman sitting across from me with patches of white running down her cheeks. "Coward," she said. Was that chalk smeared on her face? Slashes of cold cream? Did she have some incurable disease of the skin? I began to sweat. Walking home from the Cicero Avenue L stop, I thought that maybe I'd imagined her.

For months afterward, I awoke to the image of the woman's face. The simplest activities frightened me. I began to chew food very slowly, afraid I'd choke on a sliver of bone or a bite of apple or a small pea. I began to walk deliberately, fearful I'd trip on a stone or a piece of paper or my own two feet. I'd check my parents' gas stove constantly to make sure the pilot light was on. I couldn't fall asleep and spent entire nights in anxious wakefulness, sometimes getting up to look out the dining room window of my parents' spacious apartment, staring out at the empty streets. Once or twice I thought I heard the strains of piano music coming from the ceiling, a melody vaguely Debussian.

My parents were reluctant to acknowledge depression as the cause of changes in my behavior. My mother believed my problems would be solved if I married a nice Lithuanian boy with a bright future and moved to the nearby Chicago suburbs.

She even looked up the word "depression" in the English-Lithuanian Dictionary. *Įdubimas.* "A hollow," she said, "an indentation. A really big hole."

That summer I tried to keep intact my crumbling self with white wine and vodka, spending weekends with my non-Lithuanian boyfriend, Tom. I moved out of the house, against the wishes of my parents, to an apartment in Berwyn several miles away. Buying place mats and posters and coffee mugs, arranging books on an old bookcase I'd found in the alley, sneaking in a runty cat I named Mimi (after the heroine of *La Bohème*)—all these served as temporary distractions from my mental and emotional troubles. After the newness of independence wore off, I felt more miserable than before. Coffee gave me a lift; I drank gallons. When I couldn't sleep I drank wine and popped Nytols. I tried cocaine with the hope that it would stabilize my falling spirits. I called the gas company at midnight once, insisting there was a leak, I could smell it, I could feel it. The gas man came at one in the morning with a red rubberlike stick he waved back and forth like a magic wand.

"No gas," he announced.

I bought books about mental illness that focused on chemical imbalances. I considered adding genetic predisposition as another entry to the Lithuanian Dictionary of Depression, but my melancholy wasn't followed by bouts of mania; perhaps manic depression was inherited, but I wasn't so sure about hopelessness. Other books suggested vitamins and running and positive thinking as cures for persistent sadness. Nothing helped. I took a depression questionnaire in a woman's magazine; when the results suggested I seek immediate help, I dragged myself down to the Student Counseling Service at the university where I was finishing my master's degree. The administrator, alarmed at my conversations with oncoming trains, assigned me to a psychiatrist.

Dr. G. was not only a psychiatrist, but a psychoanalyst in training. Seeing an analyst as opposed to a regular therapist made me feel better immediately; I was quirky and sophisticated, a heroine in a Woody Allen movie. My elation was slightly dampened by the fact that Dr. G. looked less like an analyst, or my idea of one, than a bricklayer: stocky build, unmanicured hands, ruddy complexion.

His defining feature, however, was a black patch that covered one of his eyes. I tried my hardest to avoid gawking at his face during that first session—I stared instead at the wilting plant in the corner of his office.

"What are you trying so hard not to look at?" he asked.

"Your eye patch."

"What crosses your mind when you look at the patch?"

"Pirates," I answered.

I had the sense that Dr. G. was looking for a specific response—a big tunnel, perhaps, or an endless hole—and that I had disappointed him.

"You don't have to please me," Dr. G. said.

He suggested a parallel between my anxiety about saying the right thing and my fear of not living up to the expectations of my parents. After initial resistance to this idea, I realized I was hiding major parts of my life from my parents, highlighting those feelings and actions they would approve of.

I began to talk about Tom, whom I loved, or thought I did. I talked about how my parents looked upon the idea of my marrying Tom with as much support as if I'd told them I was joining the Young Spartacus League to ring in a new era of socialist brotherhood. I talked about how other voices, real and imaginary, present and past, joined in the chorus of disapproval. There was the famous Lithuanian priest who had survived Dachau and whose mantra reverberated through my entire being whenever I imagined myself as Wife of Tom: "It's better to marry a drunken Lithuanian than a sober American." There were the Saturday School teachers who told me that I was responsible for the continuation of the Lithuanian language, the oldest spoken European language in the world.

I talked about how a life without Tom seemed impossible—would I ever find anyone who would love me as much, who would drive me places, buy me nice dinners, keep me occupied on weekends? Yet I couldn't imagine betraying what I solemnly called My People, abandoning the ideals of my childhood, the hopes that had centered on the dream, now increasingly remote, that Lithuania would one day be free, that we could go back, we could all go back.

"Would you really want to go back?" Dr. G. asked me.

"I've never been there, so I really don't know."

"What is it that you like most about Lithuanians and Lithuanian culture?"

The idea that I had a choice in this matter—that I didn't have to buy or reject the entire package—came as a revelation. I thought about Dr. G's question over a dinner of a vodka tonic and oranges. *What is it that I like most about Lithuanians and Lithuanian culture?* I asked myself, as if taking a particularly difficult essay exam. After a second vodka tonic, I decided that I really didn't like Lithuanians very much. They were cliquish and provincial; many were racist and anti-Semitic. Their cuisine was nothing to write home about, and their national costumes made women look fat. I waited for the thunderbolt to strike, the Lithuanian Angel of Death to pay a visit. When nothing happened, I sighed in relief and poured myself more vodka.

As for the things I liked, at first nothing came to mind. Then I thought about the language, the way almost every word can be cajoled into a variation of itself, for example, *boy*: *berniukas, bernas, bernelis, bernužėlis, bernytis.* I loved Lithuanian folk songs about ducks and horses and the planting of the rue. I loved the primitive wooden sculptures of Christ the Worrier that used to dot the Lithuanian countryside before the Communists took over, though I had only seen them in books. I admired the way that earlier Lithuanians had worshipped trees and prayed for bees.

I loved Lithuanian legends, like the one about Eglė, Queen of the Snakes. The story begins as Eglė (Fir Tree) is bathing with her two older sisters in the Baltic Sea. As she dries herself off she discovers a water snake coiled in the folds of her white dress. The snake demands marriage. The sisters tell Egle to agree—after all, she can always back out. Three days later, the snake slithers down to the family's farmstead along with a posse of fellow serpents and abducts Egle, taking her down to the amber palace at the bottom of the sea. She discovers that the snake is really a handsome prince. She bears him four children, three sons and a daughter, all named after trees.

Nine years pass and Eglė begins to miss her family. She asks the Prince for permission to visit the old farmstead. He grants her a nine-day leave with the children. "How will I find my way back?" she asks. A special chant will bring him out of the waters, the Prince explains. The reunion is a happy one, though Eglė's overjoyed parents and siblings begin to wonder whether she really needs to go back. "How can she be happily married to a snake?" they ask one another. They become aware that there are special words to lure the serpent to the shore; they try to wheedle them out of the children. The brothers are firm in their resolve to keep the secret, but the daughter breaks under pressure. The family calls up the snake and kills him.

I told Dr. G. the story. We talked about the meaning of the legend, what it said about Lithuanian culture, how it related to my experiences.

"Listen to your words," Dr. G. said. *"How can she be happily married to a snake?* Who does that sound like?"

"My parents?"

"Exactly. And who do you think the snake is?"

"Tom?"

The Dictionary suddenly expanded to allow an entry for depression caused by conflicted family relationships and unrealistic cultural expectations. I continued to see Dr. G. for eight more months. I was still drinking—and reluctant to talk about my alcohol abuse; ordinary human happiness still eluded me. But my suicidal impulses disappeared, and the sense that one day I might find satisfaction in what Freud termed the cornerstones of our humanness—love and work—gave me a profound sense of hope.

Toward the end of my therapy I received and accepted a job offer from a high school in Germany to teach English. The school catered to the children of Lithuanian immigrants who'd been born in the western part of Lithuania that had once belonged to Germany.

"You're moving far away from your parents," Dr. G. commented.

"They're not very happy about that."

"And yet the high school is a Lithuanian one. The teachers and students are Lithuanian."

"Yes."

Dr. G. nodded his head slowly. I began to nod as well. We both nodded our heads for what seemed like a very long time, neither of us saying anything.

That year teaching abroad was difficult in many ways. Though the students seemed to like me, I was not an effective teacher—too lenient and eager to please. Evenings I'd drink huge glasses of beer at the local Bierstube. I still didn't drive a car. But because my parents weren't there to advise me—I couldn't call my mother every day or even weekly—I began to make my own decisions. I bought a bike and once pedaled all the way to Heidelberg, a day's journey. I took the train to Paris and Munich and Amsterdam. I broke off my relationship with Tom; I began to enjoy my own company.

That year living abroad I'd think back to the woman with the patches of white on her face. I wondered whether she was a ghost, fierce and white, visible only to me. Maybe she was my future double—a crazy homeless woman riding the trains all day. Perhaps she was my guardian angel—and the "coward" she whispered was more a warning than a taunt. She was saying I lacked courage not because I hadn't jumped but because I had left unexamined the beliefs of my parents. Fearful of the anger I might experience and the terrifying love I might find, scared of the daunting possibility of freedom, I had leapt, instead, into the widening hole of darkness.

My senior high school picture

Black Sheep

.

To say I was the black sheep of the family would be both inaccurate and slightly ridiculous—there were only two of us, and if that dubious distinction had to fall on someone, it would have certainly been my younger sister Rita, who smoked cigarettes and kept telling my father to *fuck off*. In high school she had several boyfriends, the most memorable of whom was Baker Boy, the son of the owners of Baltic Bakery. Baker Boy was a rotund, easygoing fellow who brought loaves of fresh Lithuanian rye and Latvian pumpernickel each time he came to pick my sister up. Baker Boy was followed by Opera Boy, who had little to recommend him except for the fact that he was the son of the man who sang the baritone roles in the yearly Lithuanian Opera productions. After dumping Opera Boy, my sister worked her way down the dating chain by going out with the charismatic, alcoholic son of a couple prominent in Lithuanian-American political life. My mother considered my sister's serial monogamy a sign of promiscuity—in Lithuania, girls that young simply didn't have boyfriends.

If we include extended family, then perhaps the black sheep was the beautiful cousin who drove out to California after college and never came home. She wrote songs about alienation—"the Lithuanian Joni Mitchell," her father called her—and was struck by lightning while sitting by a window ledge pondering the loveliness of a late summer storm. She survived to write a poem about it.

Or maybe the black sheep was the son of my mother's favorite brother. My oldest cousin suffered from incapacitating depressions and was prone to disturbing, inexplicable apparitions. Perhaps he was just following in the steps of his uncle, George Mačiūnas, cofounder of the Fluxus movement of modern art, long-time denizen of Greenwich Village, crazy man, paramour of Yoko Ono. Perhaps his hallucinations were brought on in part by having dropped acid throughout high school. He continued to have flashbacks for years. He spent time in an institution; then, in his late thirties he saw another, brighter, light and was baptized in the saving fire of the Holy Ghost.

My mother often talked about these two cousins, whom she felt both sorry for and condescending toward. She implied that their aberrant behavior was caused by growing up in White Plains, New York, and Western Springs, Illinois.

"This is what happens when you have too much money and live too far away from other Lithuanians," she said.

For all of my mother's criticism concerning the dissolute life of my cousins, she ignored my own destructive tendencies, especially the drinking that began when I was a sophomore in high school and ended eighteen years later. My mother couldn't acknowledge that I had a problem. Such an admission would have marred the perfect picture she had painted of me—I was her adoring daughter, her speaker of flawless Lithuanian, her scholar, her *Daivuži*. As long as I continued to love her—and got good grades and didn't tell my father to *fuck off*—she didn't see me stumbling home on weekends, didn't smell the beer or wine or peppermint schnapps on my breath or my clothes. Sometimes, driven crazy by her denial, I'd attempt a kind of partial honesty, telling her that the stress of studying for college entrance exams had finally driven me to drink; she'd bring me tea and aspirin and dry wheat toast.

My father, a recovering alcoholic and AA sponsor to several young men who'd call the house at all hours, had no delusions about my behavior. When I had to be rushed to the emergency room junior year of high school after downing a liter of Southern Comfort followed by a jug of Boone's Farm strawberry wine, topped with a sprinkling of angel dust, my father was worried but neither puzzled nor especially angry. I was his daughter, after all. Along with his hazel eyes and love of words and complete lack of physical coordination, I had inherited his fondness for booze.

After the hospitalization he told me I would have to join Alcoholics Anonymous if I wanted a chance at a decent and meaningful life. As a teenager I had no desire to live a decent and meaningful life; in fact, living a decent and meaningful life seemed to me the very definition of hell. And the idea of going to AA meetings with my dad filled me with terror. I imagined him speaking for me: "My name is Adolfas and I'm an alcoholic, and this is my daughter, Daiva. She, too, is an alcoholic." Worse, I imagined him taking a perverse pleasure at having me by his side in some moldy church basement: "Here we are, two of a kind, Father and Daughter drunks, discussing the importance of the Fifth Step."

Between my mother's denial and my father's stoic acceptance of my condition, I was free to drink with impunity. This I did, most often at any one of three bars on Sixty-Ninth Street in Marquette Park, the South Side neighborhood that in the sixties and seventies was home to the largest Lithuanian population in the Chicago area. There were bars in Cicero, of course, but they were either Mafia-run joints with the word "lounge" appended to them to suggest a marginal respectability, or depressing Lithuanian taverns where fights broke out and the chance of running into an alcoholic parent of a friend was better than average.

Marquette Park was safer, more middle-class, more solidly Lithuanian than Cicero. It was home to Holy Cross Hospital and Maria High

School, both run by the Sisters of St. Casimir, whose motherhouse on Sixty-Seventh was a red brick building with several acres of garden enclosed by a tall but graceful wrought-iron fence. The surrounding neighborhood housed several restaurants where one could order *kugelis* and *koldūnai* and, best of all, *cepelinai*, meat dumplings covered in a two-inch thick layer of potato and starch, smothered with butter and bacon bits and sour cream—Heart Attack Specials.

What mattered to me, however, were the bars, all on one street within easy walking distance of each other.

"I'm going to Sixty-Ninth Street," I'd tell my parents as friends with cars waited at the door.

"Have fun," my parents would say, as if I were going to a Sunday matinee.

The most popular of the three Lithuanian bars on Sixty-Ninth Street, at least among the younger people, was the Gintaras Club, which we called Daddy's, after the owner, whose real name remained a mystery. Daddy never carded and was quick to herd us into the basement whenever the cops raided the place. *Dar po vieną* was the motto at Daddy's. *Let's all have one more.* To the west, Lith's Club attracted the athletes, the basketball and soccer guys who played on Lithuanian intramural teams. Across the street, Playhouse exuded an atmosphere of bohemian camaraderie. It housed Antras Kaimas—Second Village—the improvisational troupe that had modeled itself on Second City. Bar-stool philosophers and would-be writers gathered at Playhouse to discuss the poetry of Janina Degutytė and the revival of ancient Lithuanian pagan rituals.

Following my parents' injunction, I *did* have fun on Sixty-Ninth Street. I had fun downing white wine at Playhouse. I had fun guzzling beer at Lith's Club. Most of all, I had fun at Daddy's. Drinks were the cheapest here, which made it the most crowded of the three bars, which made the likelihood of someone buying me my vodka tonics all the greater. If I arrived at Sixty-Ninth Street with girlfriends, I often left with some Lithuanian boy eager to have a little fun in his daddy's car.

If someone had asked me then, more than thirty years ago, why I drank, I would have answered, "Because it makes me feel good." I loved the sensation of cold white wine rushing down my throat, of icy-smooth vodka lingering on my tongue. My muscles would relax; words that had lain nestled somewhere in the frontal cortex of my brain would begin to flow as freely as the beer on tap at Daddy's. I suppose I drank to escape "the bondage of self," as they say in AA, though I didn't have the powers of self-reflection at sixteen to make the connection between my eagerness to get wasted and the shyness that was so prominent an aspect of my personality. I struggled to enter conversations at parties, especially Lithuanian ones, baffled by the unspoken rules that signified rank. I felt more comfortable on stage reciting Lithuanian poetry in front of critical listeners than exchanging a few words with a stranger.

The idea that I could, or should, limit or even pace my drinks was as foreign to me as putting money into U.S. Savings Bonds: I drank to get drunk. Sometimes the end result was a kind of dumbstruck happiness that left me staring openmouthed at the wonderfully unpredictable world around me. Other times a frightening sensation of weightlessness would overtake me; I'd wake up having forgotten what I had said and done the night before. The first time this had happened I'd been scared enough to talk about it with my father.

"A curtain of darkness slowly descended over everything," I told him dramatically. "It lifted for a moment or two, only to come crashing down again."

"We call those blackouts," answered my father matter-of-factly.

When I look over the written evidence of my life during those early years of drinking, the birthday cards and vacation letters I'd received from friends, the yearbook inscriptions, I'm struck by how often the word *nice* appears: "For you, just for being so nice," "You are truly one of the nicest people I know," "Stay as nice as you are." Perhaps this was a universal adjective for young women growing up in the early seventies in America—

one was either nice or not, and the not-nice girls simply didn't have friends who sent them birthday cards or scribbled in their yearbooks.

What perplexes me about these chronicles of pleasantry is that I don't remember myself as being nice. I remember myself as angry, angry because I wasn't slim enough to play the ingénue in the high school play, angry because my shyness prevented me from asking questions in class, angry because I couldn't spike a volleyball or do a side-split in gym. I was angry, as well, with my parents, because they wouldn't let me go away to college. I had dreamed of a small, private school somewhere in Minnesota or Iowa. "We don't have the money," my parents had said—and this was true—but they were also afraid that I would fall in love with an American boy and never come home. If the local state university, a convenient L ride away, was good enough for all of the other young Lithuanians, it was good enough for me.

Had I been able to express some of this anger instead of submerging it in alcohol, I could have protested more forcefully, could have applied for scholarships, promised to take on more jobs. In the end, however, I don't know if it would have mattered. My grades were barely above average; I had C's in chemistry and advanced algebra, and hadn't even taken calculus and physics. My ACT scores were schizophrenic, suggesting an individual who stayed up nights reading old dictionaries but still counted on her fingers. And although I earned money summers and during Christmas break waitressing or selling shoes, I wasn't willing to work during the school year—a job would take away from both my study time and my drinking.

I ended up taking the L to the university where I threw myself into Victorian novels and Romantic poetry and the arms of men I barely knew. I'd be sitting outside at a picnic table, reading, sucking on a straw, a sweater thrown over some flimsy dress, or in the cafeteria drinking cup after cup of coffee when a boy in a Doors t-shirt or a man in a goatee would approach me: *You look familiar. Weren't you in my chemistry class? What are you reading?*

Junior year I fell in love with Tom, eleven years my senior. I had met him at a small party thrown by my future brother-in-law. Emboldened by a few drinks, prompted by my confidence in reading the body language of men—I was an expert at interpreting looks from mildly interested to highly intrigued, from unavailable to willing-but-shy—I sidled up to him like a cat, rubbing my leg against his. I might have even purred.

Tom was handsome in a broad-shouldered, big-handed kind of way. Even his Germanic last name, translated into English, signified strength: Breaker of Stone. What I loved about him had as much to do with his looks as with the fact that he was smart and sophisticated, an architect with an MA in German. He introduced me to the architecture of Mies van der Rohe, whom he referred to simply as Mies, as if they were old buddies. He introduced me to good wine, to vintages and bouquets. I smacked my lips and acted as if I understood the fine gradations and varying aftertastes. I got drunk less often with Tom than I'd had with other boyfriends, though I still needed alcohol to navigate simple everyday activities.

It was with Tom that I saw the first fireworks of my life. We sat on cool metal benches at the local high school and drank beer out of large plastic cups and listened to the band play Sousa marches. The fireworks left me breathless. They rocketed up into the sky with such force I thought they would pierce the clouds and zoom right through heaven. I loved their delicacy, the way they dissolved into the air, leaving behind for a second or two the ghost of their impressions.

Tom took me to the first baseball game of my life. I dressed as if I were going to Sunday Mass— high-heeled sandals, flowered dress, little straw clutch. The White Sox lost to Boston by two runs. Carlton Fisk, the handsome catcher for the White Sox, got a round of applause mingled with boos—he'd played for the Red Sox the previous year. I spilled beer on my dress and pestered Tom with questions:

"Why are we clapping?"

"That was a pop-up."

"A pop-up?"

"It's a high ball that's easily caught."

"A high ball? I always thought those were drinks," I said, laughing at my own lame joke.

"You're too young," my father said when I mentioned marrying Tom, though my sister had gotten married at nineteen.

"Think of what Christmases will be like. We'll all have to speak English. English for *his* sake," said my mother, as if English was some obscure aboriginal dialect way beyond their comprehension.

I broke up with Tom several times over the course of four years, returning to him when I felt lonely or sad, feeling guilty about my behavior.

It was during one of these breaks that I met my first husband, a Lithuanian by way of Canada. He was a friend of the groom's at a Cicero wedding; the bride had been a classmate of mine. People kept asking her whether she'd keep her maiden name—not out of any newfangled feminist beliefs, but because she was a Radvilaitė—a Radziwill— descended from the same bloodlines as the prince of Monaco, who we all knew was of Lithuanian ancestry and whose forefathers had only changed their surnames through forced Polonization sometime in the sixteenth century.

The wedding was held at the church hall of St. Anthony's; tables used for bingo were covered with white tablecloths, streamers drooping across the makeshift dance floor were fastened to columns by clusters of balloons. I watched my future husband leading the younger wedding guests in a circle dance, pulling everyone around the hall in ever-increasing speed. All of a sudden, mid-music, he stopped. A few of the dancers collapsed into him, landing on the floor.

"Time for more drinks," he shouted in Lithuanian. Everyone laughed as if something funny had been said.

He flirted with me later in the evening. I didn't find him particularly attractive. His blond hair was a mess of sweaty curls; his pale skin flushed an apple-pink, as if some grandma had pinched his cheeks too roughly. But he was attentive and generous. He made my own drinking seem like an amateur enterprise, something I might get really good at some day with enough practice and persistence.

We drank our way across three continents, settling for a time in the Middle East, in Saudi Arabia, a country where alcohol is illegal. This didn't stop us from paying hundreds of dollars for black-market booze. We made our own alcohol as well, buying ten pound bags of sugar and six-bottle cases of grape juice at the Riyadh Safeway, exchanging sly smiles with other Westerners in line with the same items.

My relationship with him ended the same way it began, at a Lithuanian wedding. I woke up the next morning recalling the final moments of the night, standing at the bar with a wine glass in my hand, arguing with the bartender who was packing up. The closing of the bar at two a.m. at a Lithuanian reception seemed to me to be the height of unreasonable behavior.

"Ish ludiculous," I said.

When he wouldn't listen, I wandered from table to table, a well-dressed woman of thirty-three, pouring leftover wine from half-empty glasses into one large water tumbler, my own super-sized goblet, my personal Biggie Wine.

That morning my husband and I looked at each other and realized that we didn't know how we'd gotten home. We couldn't remember who had driven the red Audi Fox we'd purchased just months before or where we had parked it—my husband went outside to investigate. As I combed the vomit from my hair so it wouldn't clump when I took a shower something inside me shattered, some long-held resistance to a life of normalcy. I was so sick I could barely reach for the phone to dial the operator and ask, in a neutral-sounding voice—as if I were requesting the number of the local China Buffet—for the main Chicago listing of Alcoholics Anonymous.

Perhaps it was the will of an angry God that had yanked me out of bed and onto the cool wooden floor where I found myself on my knees, like Paul off his horse on the way to Damascus. More likely it was the echo of my father's voice—he'd been dead a year—that had guided my trembling hand to the phone. This is what *he* had done. This is what had worked for *him*.

In the coming months I searched the basement meeting rooms of AA for his ghost, who was there in the presence of the people who had known him; they talked about him with fondness and respect. "You're his daughter?" they sometimes asked, less in surprise than in polite curiosity.

My mother remained skeptical of my newfound zeal, jealous of my new community.

"Why don't you just drink a little less?" she suggested politely.

At some point in my sobriety I stopped viewing my addiction to alcohol as a character flaw enhanced by genetics to understanding it as a national characteristic, one that my fellow countrymen had either ignored or viewed as a troublesome but almost charming trait, aligning Lithuania with larger, more famous countries like Ireland whose poets raise their glasses to every heroic utterance, whose bards continue telling stories even as they stumble home down country roads.

Because so many of the Lithuanians around me drank, and because I'd spent the greater part of my life in their presence, I had assumed that this is what most adults living in the United States did—they drank at weddings and funerals and christenings, during holidays and holy days, at banquets and picnics and dances. They drank and they got drunk and then they burst into song.

I suppose on some level I knew that alcohol was part of my cultural heritage, as expected as the Lithuanian national anthem during Vasario 16 meetings, as familiar as borscht. "You Lithuanians, you can really put 'em down," an acquaintance told me once. He was Irish-American, the son of alcoholics. But it was only when I quit drinking that I realized, after a few first awkward sorties into social gatherings, that the great majority of Americans stopped at two or three glasses of wine or beer—I could easily turn down an offer of a drink by simply saying "no."

It was much harder saying "no" to Lithuanians. While many of my Lithuanian friends were supportive of my decision to abstain completely, others viewed it as an aberration, even a betrayal of sorts.

"What's *wrong* with you?" they asked.

It was worse when I traveled to Lithuania, several years after the collapse of the Soviet Union. At lunch at the home of relatives in Vilnius, I saw that alongside a buffet of pickled herring, pickled mushrooms, dark brown bread, farmer's cheese, three types of sausage, and deep-fried chicken cutlets there was an entire table just for booze: wine and champagne and beer and a whiskey called Bobelinė, named after Kazys Bobelis, a retired physician from Florida in his seventies who had pretensions to public office in Lithuania.

"How come they named this after him?" I asked my great-aunt Irena.

"He appeared on TV one day, some interview program, and the host asked him the secret of his health. He held up a glass of whiskey. 'I drink this every day,' he said. 'And so should you.'"

I tried to imagine an American politician—Hillary Clinton or Al Gore or even George W. Bush—going on the air and picking up a glass of whiskey and telling the viewing audience: "I drink this every day and so should you."

My aunt poured me a glass.

"No thank you," I said.

"But you must," she said.

"But I can't," I answered.

"But you must."

"I'm taking medication. Strong medication. Mixed with alcohol, it can cause death."

My relatives stared at me openmouthed.

"Well, then have some more pickled herring," said my aunt.

◦◦◦◦◦◦◦◦◦◦◦◦◦

My mother and I are sitting in her Oak Lawn condo, sipping black tea out of large ceramic mugs. She complains about the weight of the mugs; she, who has always loved their modern sculptural quality, now longs for smaller, more delicate vessels. I am reluctant to tell her I'll buy her a set. "What for?" she'll say. "I won't be around much longer." Instead I ask if she'd like a shot of "special" degtinė from a bottle brimming with magical herbs and enough alcohol to rid a hospital of bacteria. But not enough to kill the cancer cells that keep spreading through her body, oblivious to chemo and radiation and special prayers for the sick at Sunday Mass.

"Sure," she says.

"I'm going to abstain, mom," I say, as she tries to pour me a drink.

"I'm so glad that you stopped drinking. I always knew you had a problem, but you just wouldn't listen. The stubbornness of the young, I suppose."

"Mom, I drank until I was thirty-three."

"You got it from your dad's side," she says, ignoring an uncle for whom several shots of vodka and two or three beers were rewards for a hard day's work.

I tell her of what I've read in an online article on worldwide alcoholism rates: Lithuania tops the list. I wait for her to deny this the way she dismisses so many other unpleasant facts that don't agree with the way she views the world.

"At least we're number one in something," says my mother.

My grandmother with my mother (*left*)
and her brother, Jurgis

The Alphabet of Silence

On my mother's otherwise bald head, a few wisps of white hair stand up like the fur of some surprised alley cat. Her ears seem huge. With her large blue-gray eyes, her skin, remarkably smooth for eighty-four, the wrinkles on her face congregating primarily along her mouth, she looks like Yoda.

My mother has never seen *Star Wars*.

"Please stop calling me Yoda," she says.

"But Yoda's a wise man. A seer."

"Most people are see-ers. The number of blind people on this earth is quite small."

We are in my mother's study, surrounded by cardboard containers of varying sizes, half-empty suitcases, file folders stuffed with letters and greeting cards, stacks of old newspapers.

My mother hands me a big brown box.

"Here," she says. "They're yours. I can't do anything with them."

They are photographs, and there are hundreds and hundreds of them. "I keep meaning to organize them, but, well, you know how I am."

My mother has seen my wedding scrapbook. She knows the hours I've spent choosing photographs, cutting, cropping, organizing, buying fancy papers at special stores. Surely she doesn't expect a similar endeavor?

"They're yours to *keep*," she says, reading my mind. Then: "How long do you think I'm going to be around, anyway?"

"I don't know, mom. I'm not a doctor."

"Doctors, they don't know anything."

"Okay, I'm not God."

"God," she harrumphs, throwing up her hands.

Her ambivalence over the existence of a Supreme Being has grown in the past year or two. When my friend Terese came to visit, she brought, in addition to blueberry soup and apple pancakes from Bobek's Delicatessen, a prayer book dedicated to St. Rita, the patron of impossible causes. My mother turned to me and laughed.

"Yes, your sister Rita. She has long been an impossible cause."

My mother accepts the prayers of others, but finds it difficult to pray herself.

"Do you know what I want?" she asks.

"What do you want?"

"Ten more years. Ten more good years."

"What would you do with the ten good years?"

"Go to Spain."

Spain?

At the top of the box, more recent photos—a trip to Rome with my father for the five hundredth anniversary of the birth of St. Casimir, one to the Caribbean with her brother Jurgis and his wife Nijolė. There are pictures taken by my mother that she proudly calls "artistic." My mother's sense of perspective and attention to detail are superb. But the pictures are shot with a cheap Kodak from the seventies, and the subject matter never strays from the commonplace and traditional: a vase of roses, a tree outside her picture window, the Trevi fountain, the Eiffel Tower.

In the middle are photos from the distant past: my mother on skis, smiling, ready to take on the world; my mother surrounded by a group of young men vying for her favors; my mother in profile, looking very Greta Garbo–like—eyebrows arched, a beige fedora pulled rakishly over her face.

At the very bottom are childhood photos. Here she is—a sullen, dark-eyed little girl. Here, a proper young lady, dark hair cropped at the chin, a bow the size of a large bird, wings spread, perched atop her head. There are portraits of her parents; her father, professorial, unsmiling; her mother, elegant, dimpled. There are photographs of my mother's childhood friends, girls from good families, families like my mother's, city girls who played the piano and vacationed in Palanga.

Most of the photographs are not labeled, existing in a cosmic universe unmoored from time or place. A black-and-white photograph of my grandfather standing on what looks like an iceberg. There are no icebergs in Lithuania.

"Mom, where was this taken?"

"I don't know. Switzerland maybe."

My mother's hours of darkness and fear have been punctuated by moments of lightness and grace. She brags about my sister's new job as fund-raiser for a major university; she has rejoiced over my cousin's new baby; most of all, she celebrates my marriage to Marty. That she had the strength to walk me down the aisle, give me away to the man of my dreams, has been a major accomplishment.

Although half a year has passed, she talks about the wedding every time I see her, how perfect it was, how happy I looked: "There was none of the false cheer of your first big event. And so much more tasteful." Instead of a small Lithuanian orchestra grinding out polkas, a string quartet played Vivaldi. Instead of *kugelis* and sausage, there was salmon and asparagus. Instead of a billowing gown and voluminous veil, I wore an empire-waist Italian dress and tiny pearl tiara. At forty-six I looked better, more relaxed, more myself—younger, if that's possible—than I did at twenty-eight. And instead of throwing my bouquet of scarlet roses over my shoulder for unmarried friends to catch, I handed it grandly to my mother. She stretched her arms out to take the flowers, then smiled and waved her hand back and forth, as if she had just been crowned the new Miss America.

I take the photos down to the car, along with several of my father's old notebooks, a book of Lithuanian maps, and an aging ficus in a brown ceramic planter.

When I come back, my mother hands me a box of silverware, forks and spoons and knives tarnished with age, heavier than any I have ever handled. The letter B is inscribed on each individual piece with a graceful flourish.

"Here," she says. "I thought you might want these."

The last time I had seen the silverware I was in the seventh grade. I had been at the Cicero Public library, looking at books on modern European history, attempting to supplement the education I had been receiving from the nuns. That day I did what I usually did—I checked the book's index under *L—L* for Lithuania, to see if anyone had cared to write about my little country. Someone had, but my elation turned quickly into shock. The book talked about the Nazi invasion of Lithuania—which I had known about—and the fact that more than 90 percent of the Jews had been exterminated, which I had not. The author stressed that the Nazis could not have accomplished the goal by themselves, and that many Lithuanians had participated in the executions. "I question this," I wrote in pencil on the page, my first adult marginalia. Later that evening, I asked my mother about the Lithuanian participation. I expected her to say something about the inaccuracy of history books written by Americans, something she often did—but she just brought out the box.

"The B is for Berenstein. Dr. Berenstein was our family physician," my mother had said. "When the Nazis occupied Klaipėda, Dr. Berenstein gave the silver to your grandfather, for safekeeping."

"Mom, why did you hold on so long to this?" I question.

"I don't know. I thought that maybe one day Dr. Berenstein would return."

"What am I supposed to do?" I ask, my voice rising. "Use these forks and knives and spoons for Sunday brunch?"

She frowns and on her face I see the old, familiar look: I am scolding her.

I think back to the Jewish Museum in Vilnius, when the woman at the desk asked me where I was from. "Chicago," I said. *Chicago* she wrote down slowly in a large black book and then looked at me and asked, in a voice almost unbearably kind, whether I'd be interested in visiting the exhibit upstairs honoring Lithuanians who had rescued Jews during the Nazi occupation: "You can skip the other floors if you like and go straight to the Hall of the Righteous."

I wanted to see the other exhibits and wandered from floor to floor, reflecting on the photographs and paintings and Hebrew manuscripts, on the life that unfolded before me like a finely woven prayer rug. Because Lithuanian Jews had been written out of the history books that I'd read in Lithuanian Saturday School, because they had never been mentioned in the seminars on Lithuanian culture that I attended, the idea that our Nemunas was their river as well, that they had hated the czars just as we had, that they summered by the Baltic Sea and loved pickled herring and potato pancakes just as we did came as an almost biblical revelation.

The Hall of the Righteous consisted of two little rooms with photographs of the Savers. An adjacent room contained a large map with dozens of triangles marking villages and cities where Jews had been massacred.

"You know the Jewish Museum in Vilnius?" I ask my mother.

"What about the Jewish Museum?"

"I was the only person there."

"So? Maybe the owners charged too much for admission."

"Admission was free."

"Your grandmother saved a Jewish family."

"I know the story."

In Kaunas during the Nazi occupation, my grandmother had sheltered a Jewish mother and her son. My mother remembers measuring out curtains. She remembers the boy, who begged to play outside, and the mother, who had been a dentist.

"Your grandmother gave her some mending to do, thinking, well, she must have good hands. But she turned out to be a poor mender. A really poor mender."

"That's the only time you, or *anybody*, ever talked about the Jews."

"*Not* the only time."

"Nobody ever discussed the Holocaust. It was always the Russians, the Russians, the Russians. They did this and this and this to us."

"Your grandmother could have gotten all of us killed by her actions. Your grandfather was furious. He came home one day to find these strangers settled in our apartment. Your grandparents argued for weeks. Quietly, of course."

"Why did she do it?"

"Why did she do it?" my mother repeats this question. "Because she hated the Nazis. And because she felt sorry for the little boy."

My mother is on the verge of tears.

"Don't you have any happy memories of childhood?" she asks.

She wants assurance that she was a good mother. I squeeze her hand and tell her that I love her, that, yes, she has been a good mother.

"I know I was a good mother. But what was the *best* thing I did?"

"You always encouraged me to do my best."

"Every mother did that."

"You loved me."

"That's a mother's job."

"You made me speak Lithuanian."

She smiles and nods her head.

I try to tell her that the fact that I can navigate the world with two languages, two cultures, two voices, one to critique the other, is a constant good, but my Lithuanian fails me once again.

Instead, I hug her, hold her for a very long time to prevent her from dissolving in my arms, from disappearing into the air.

My father and I

Unfinished Symphony

My father told me once, out of the blue, that he had been a cook for the Germans during the occupation. Because he'd left it at that, for years I thought he had willfully joined the Nazis. The fact that his first name was Adolfas added to the evidence compiling in my head. I lived ashamed of his secret past, fearful of the day when proof of his atrocities would come to light, his photograph plastered across the front page of the *Chicago Tribune*. I didn't realize that my father hated his name, would correct his American employers when they called him Adolph: "It's Aaah-dolfas," he'd drawl.

Years later I learned about forced labor, from my mother, of course, and realized what had happened to my father.

"They *made* you cook, didn't they?" I asked.

Although my father had cooked for the Nazis, at home he couldn't scramble an egg. He asked where we kept the spoons. He would summon my mother to get the horseradish when he was sitting next to the refrigerator. He claimed not to know how to use an iron. One of my first childhood tasks was to iron his handkerchiefs, dozens of them. They had to be starched and perfectly pressed and folded carefully into neat little squares. A singed corner or poorly creased edge provoked a string of Lithuanian obscenities.

My father cursed missing tie clips and plastic bags that wouldn't open and cheaply manufactured staplers. *Šūdo vaikas*, he'd call the tie clip or the plastic bag or the stapler. *Child of shit.* Occasionally he ventured into English language profanities; *son mubba bitch* was his favorite. The tenant late with the rent was a son mubba bitch, as was the editor who'd omitted my father's name from the Encyclopedia of Lithuanian Writers in Exile. And my sister, when she used up all the film in his camera, was definitely a son mubba bitch.

My mother, except for the occasional *JēzusMaria* strung together to express disgust, rarely swore. She talked a lot, however. I know that in Regensburg she'd had a premonition of when the bombs would fall; she stayed inside that day. On the journey to the United States she'd boasted to the U.S. navy men about her glamorous destination: "I'm going to Brooklyn!" she exclaimed, throwing back her hair. I know that she had wanted to be an architect, that she resented her mother's meddling in her private life.

The only time my father talked about his family was in relation to his father's drinking. His father would beat him with a thick black belt, making him kiss the leather strap before each whack.

"This was the way things were done in Dusetos," my father would say, without rancor.

My father never hit me with a thick black belt; he rarely touched me. My sister more often bore the brunt of my father's temper. Whereas I was quiet, internalizing everything around me, Rita was quick to anger, impulsive, temperamental. By the time she was fifteen years old she was two inches taller than my fifty-five-year-old father and almost as heavy.

An unflushed toilet, an overdue library book would send my father into a rage. *Šūdo vaikas*, my father would yell. *Fuck you*, my sister would answer. *Fuck you*. Like two springs suddenly uncoiled, they would flail about for a minute, hands in the air, then, almost as if by accident, converge upon each other, pushing and yelling.

She moved out of the house at eighteen, an unheard of age in our Lithuanian community. She married at nineteen.

I once told a Lithuanian friend from the neighborhood about my father's temper, his behavior toward my sister. She shrugged: "They were *all* like that."

My father took pride in my accomplishments—my good grades, the leads in high school plays, my perfect Lithuanian enunciation—a pride coupled with almost complete ignorance of who I was as a person. He didn't know I loved Bob Dylan and J. R. R. Tolkien. He didn't know I thought my feet were too big and that I was scared of heights and that I desperately wanted a boyfriend.

There were times we connected, briefly, tenuously. He took ballroom dancing classes with my mother, who was a good dancer, who loved to dance. I was his partner once or twice when my mother couldn't make it. He struggled with simple waltzes, shifting his weight from one foot to another, hopping back and forth like Yul Brynner in the "Shall We Dance?" sequence from the *King and I*. In me he had a partner of almost equal gracelessness. I couldn't follow my father's lead, afraid I'd step on his toes. He was reluctant to take charge. The only dance we could manage was the polka.

When I was failing driver's ed in high school, my father would take me driving on Sunday mornings, early Sunday mornings, six o'clock Sunday mornings. He said this was the best time. "No cars on road," he'd explain. We took Cermak Road down to the Oak Brook shopping center, where we drove around and around the empty parking lot. Then we drove home. After a few Sundays I grew tired of this. I was seventeen and all of my boyfriends had cars. I did not want to get up at 5 a.m. to go driving with my father. More than that, though, I was afraid that he would start yelling at me, would criticize my attempts at parallel parking, would call me *šūdo vaikas*.

Then there was the time I was twenty and reciting poetry at one of the Friday literature evenings in the basement café of the Lithuanian Center. I loved one poem above the others, written by Justinas Marcinkevičius in the secret language of poets living under the occupation. During the refrain—*you wood of cradle, wood of coffin*—the words stuck in my throat. I had to stop. I looked out at the audience and saw that my father, too, was crying. My mother came up to me after the reading. She picked a hair off of my black woolen dress. She told me that the Mackus was read just a little too quickly. Everything else was fine. My anger at her—for whom did I do these readings if not for her—was leavened by the tenderness I felt at that moment for my father.

When I was eight years old my father stopped drinking. The incident that had propelled this life-changing event was a car accident. We were coming home from a Lithuanian event in Marquette Park when ice on the Cicero Avenue overpass caused the wheels of my father's light blue Falcon to lock and skid. The car swerved into and over a concrete railing. We hung suspended between life and death, my mother yelling, my sister wailing, me reciting a perfect Act of Contrition as the nuns had instructed us to do in cases like this, my father slumped over the steering wheel, drunk and stunned and scared and remorseful.

Along with my father's newfound sobriety came a long-repressed burst of creativity. Perhaps the stories he told at AA meetings inspired him to begin to write again. Several evenings a week and on Saturday mornings he'd sit in front of an old silvery Smith-Corona, getting words down on paper, a phrase, a sentence at a time, until a page would fill up and then another page. After a few days, or a week, or a month, a story would emerge, about a fish he caught in Lake Zarasai or a prank he played on his best friend in the Displaced Persons camp in Salzburg.

A small Lithuanian press in Chicago published his collection, titled *The Unfinished Symphony*. A leading critic for *Draugas* headlined his review: "A Dozen Good Stories."

A reporter from the *Cicero Life* came to interview us. "One Family's Story: Immigrants Caught between Two Cultures," the headline read.

"I am famous because I have a famous family," my mother is quoted in the story.

In the accompanying photograph my mother's head is bowed. She seems to have gotten smaller. My father is turned away from the camera. I am also in profile, sullen and dramatic. The only one smiling is my sister, as if there is something very amusing about this whole business, the family so unnaturally posed around a piece of pagan sculpture—a tall wooden folk Madonna I had received for a sixteenth birthday present. The photographer had wanted us grouped around the family piano, sheet music in hand, ready for a sing-along. "We never gather around the piano," my sister informed him curtly. "We never sing together."

When I was in graduate school my father wanted me to translate a story from *The Unfinished Symphony*. He wanted to send it to the *New Yorker*. I had been writing for a few years, getting used to rejection, letters from the editors of literary magazines that said the same thing over and over again on crudely xeroxed slips of paper. A few were handwritten, offering suggestions or encouragement. I saved these like pretty colored stones found on the beach among big ugly brown ones, placing them in a little metal box. One was from the *New Yorker*.

I told my father I couldn't translate his story. There were problems of translation I was unequipped to handle: metaphors, prepositional phrases, the adverbial frequentative past.

When I was in my late twenties and working overseas in Saudi Arabia, living with my then husband, my father began to write me long and frequent letters, perfectly typed—so different from my mother's almost unreadable scrawl—composed in flawless, literary Lithuanian.

Today, Memorial Day, the rain is coming down and the radiators are heating up and I am writing you this letter, well, not knowing what to write. We miss you very much, Daivute. . . . Maybe Memorial Day isn't the very best time to talk about the living, but we always think of you, in hours of both joy and sorrow. Of course, we don't have very many really sorrowful hours, unless your mother and I have a fight, although at our age sadness seems to come unexpectedly, like a wind from who knows what direction. There are daily joys, though. Not having to work any longer, for one. It seems one can live quite happily without work.

Reading these letters, I was taken aback by their personal nature, by my father's sense of intimacy. He never spoke this way in real life: "We miss you very much." He never used the diminutive of my name, "Daivute," in everyday conversation.

I've taken a break here and, after four days, am trying to write again. As you know, it's not always easy to express one's thoughts. . . . I'm thinking that I will write and tell you that today is very cold. Last night the temperature hovered below zero. The windows have frozen over, and it's good to be inside, sitting in a warm room, listening to music and thinking about summer, listening to Beethoven's Sixth Symphony with its cuckoo's call, daydreaming about childhood, when my brother and I—the brother killed in Vorkuta—would, in the darkness of snowy evening, sneak off to the public forest to steal a Christmas tree. We would chop it down and, in the night, drag it home on a sled. Our ears would redden from the cold. Shaking off the snow, we would haul the tree into our house and light the only candle we had, the "grabnyčia," used when someone died. Oh, what Christmas joy, and without ornaments or wreaths or cookies!

I was filled, on the one hand, with a sense that I had misread my father. I had never fully understood him, had never taken the time to ask, to listen. On the other hand, I felt the old familiar rage welling up inside, rising slowly to the surface.

Today we got your letter, which your mother, as always, read with tears in her eyes, frequently reminding me of my insensitivity to my children. In reality, she doesn't think that way, but I have to admit she is more sensitive than I am, and, like all mothers, more sensitive than fathers, who don't have the bond of childbirth to tie them to their children.

My father's belief that women are naturally closer to their children was expressed often enough that I had brought it up in therapy years before as an excuse for his distance. My therapist talked about the many loving fathers he knew, and the many distant indifferent mothers.

I wrote back to my father about life in Saudi Arabia. In broken Lithuanian I told him how the diminishing light at dusk made me think of the famous line from "Prufrock" about the evening "spread out against the sky / like a patient etherized upon a table"; how students at the university loved to touch my "golden" hair; how lonely I often felt. It was perhaps the first and last time I communicated with him so eagerly and honestly, with little hesitation and no regrets.

When my father was diagnosed with stomach cancer at sixty-seven, I took a leave of absence from my teaching job in Saudi Arabia and a corresponding separation from my husband to help nurse my father. I wiped the dribble from his chin and tried to feed him chicken broth and crackers. Little things gave him pleasure—watching a fishing show on television, listening to a favorite piece of music, a Shubert symphony or a string quartet by Brahms.

A few weeks before he died, the Lithuanian daily *Draugas* published an essay of my father's in its Saturday cultural supplement. Titled "Father," the work begins with a long and detailed physical description of my father's father—my grandfather—who died before I was born:

> I see him in the parish hall, his small head tilted forwards, listening to the words of the speaker as if gazing out at distant birches, or at the black stripe of forest in the horizon swaying in the summer wind above the blossoming fields of wheat, a mist of pollen rising out of that billowing boundless breadth. Solitary, shadowy, mute. It's as if somebody else was sitting there in the third row—an apparition in a black suit. Shrunken, exhausted. That's the way he might have appeared just after the First World War, back from German captivity. . . . I can almost see him: his narrow little tie, a spattered coat that once fit a much heavier man, trousers with hollowed knees, trousers that never saw an iron. He sat colorless, without emotion, the hair on the top of his head like the quills on a porcupine, his small head raised in order to better hear and

remember the words of the speaker concerning the significance of Lithuanian Independence Day.

I was surprised by the number of people who packed the Petkus Funeral Home—extra chairs had to be provided for the service; some people had to stand in the back. Delegates from various Lithuanian organizations talked about my father. I watched the representative of the Frontininkai as he tripped over the microphone wire going up to give yet another speech. His elegant white-haired wife, sitting in the front row, scowled. I cried neither at the service, nor at the burial. St. Casimir's Cemetery, which I had always thought so beautiful, with its stone angels and graceful metal crosses and tombstones dating back to when the letter *w* existed in Lithuanian, looked like someone's gaudy, oversized backyard. I fiddled with the thick faux-leather belt of the black polyester dress I had bought that week and looked around at the faces of relatives I hadn't seen in years, wondering if they noticed that I had gained weight. As the priest intoned the final prayer and the Lithuanian anthem was sung and the coffin was lowered into the parched August ground, all I could think of was how badly I wanted a drink.

Several weeks later, I took out the essay my father had written about his own father, published in *Draugas* just a few months back. I carefully unfolded the newspaper and looked at the photograph of my father in his thick dark glasses and tweed jacket, looking like an academic. As I sat on the bed with only a dim night lamp for light, my father's life disclosed itself through the letters on the page. I hadn't known that his father had been sentenced to ten years of hard labor in Vorkuta for owning a gun, that his wife and youngest son had been deported to another region. I hadn't known that his father died of pneumonia brought on by starvation and cold. I hadn't even known that the location of my grandfather's grave remains a mystery, the bones intact in ground perpetually frozen, unmarked by a cross or stone.

The greatest revelation had to do not with hardships and political events, but with the affection that my father shows his father, a tenderness that suffuses the work, a longing free of anger or resentment, an attachment that, if one looks closely and reads between the lines, almost resembles love:

> I would see him, sitting in the parish hall, the third row. I know neither how he made his way in nor how he snuck out. Perhaps like a dream, without the slightest shuffling of shoes. Like a wingless black bird, like an extended shadow in the light of the stars. He was my father.

I cried for my father and his unfinished dreams. I cried for all of the words he had never spoken, for all the questions I had never asked.

Our Lady of the Gates of Dawn in Vilnius

Black Marija

I am driving south on Halsted Street, passing the university that has granted me my doctorate, passing the former Maxwell Street Market, recently demolished to make way for university parking. A hundred years ago Eastern European Jews set up their carts here, peddling buttons and goat's milk and herring and coal. As late as the 1990s, African American merchants sold used tires, portraits of Martin Luther King and Malcolm X, gold-plated pendants, and the best french fries in Chicago.

I drive past the Amber House: Ladie's [*sic*] and Men's Clothes, the East Breeze Cafe, the Romuva movie theater. I stop, briefly, at the old International Amphitheater, which formed part of the eastern border of what used to be the Stockyards, and roll down my windows to sniff for smells I associate with the Lithuanian dance festivals held there every four years in the fifties and sixties—decaying meat mingled with human perspiration. Dressed in a heavy woolen skirt and a long-sleeved linen blouse, my hair in chunky braids, I would wait impatiently with the rest of the Saturday School contingent from St. Anthony's to dance the Gyvataras. I remember the sky as yellow, the dancers from exotic far-away cities—Toronto, Detroit—piling out of yellow buses.

The Stockyards have been closed for more than four decades. The air smells of gasoline and cheap wine. I turn west on Fifty-Fifth, or Garfield Boulevard, a boulevard of solid gray-stones that in another neighbor-hood would run into the millions. I make a right on Ashland, and pass the O.K. Shoes and Street Life Clothes, the Golly Box Company and the ghost of the building that used to be a Goldblatt's—only the sign remains. I turn left onto an unnamed street.

This is not the most efficient route to my mother's condominium in Oak Lawn. I am meandering, a habit of mine when I don't want to con-front unpleasant realities. I turn right and keep going for several blocks. I make a left onto an unnamed street; a group of boys enthusiastically point to a no left turn sign. By the time I make another left I am lost in the Back of the Yards, a neighborhood without a real name. The "back" suggests that we are not even "in" something, but on its margins. In Up-ton Sinclair's 1906 novel *The Jungle*, the area is Packingtown, a designa-tion no less symbolic; the laborers not only pack meat into containers for eventual sale, but are packed themselves into living spaces too small for human habitation. In the 1900s, many of the boarding house owners were Lithuanian, as were most of the tavern keepers. According to one historical source, saloons would sprout up in the Back of the Yards "like mushrooms after rain."

In the surrounding neighborhood, a placard advertises Back of the Yards Cool Heat—"Everything for Your Air-conditioning Needs," one of the few signs in English. One rarely sees "Se Habla Espanol" on storefronts or restaurants—it is clear that everybody speaks Spanish here. The Contreras Lounge and a *lave rápido* and the many *carniceras* and *fruterias* and *mercados* are evidence of this. A billboard of Snoopy, that most American of dogs, proclaims "Seguro de Vida." It is an adver-tisement for Metropolitan Life Insurance, and shows Snoopy smartly dressed in a business suit, carrying a briefcase. The bold black lettering of the sign contrasts with the graffiti found on the surrounding streets: you see it everywhere, on mailboxes and stop signs, on steel garage doors and brick walls: The Almighty Saints Rule.

Ninety years ago the signs advertising clothing stories, grocery shops, and saloons would have been in Lithuanian. Today, one remaining relic is carved in granite—Eudeikis Funeral Home; another is printed on aluminum—the words Baltic Bakery spelled in black against a mustard-yellow background. The funeral home has been transformed into a residence, but the bakery shows signs of life—a delivery man carries trays of freshly baked bread into a truck pulled into the driveway.

I drive a few more blocks north and west and then I see it, Holy Cross Church, *Švento Kryžiaus Bažnyčia*, an orange brick baroque building with a white concrete rim of frosting. I've been to Mass here once, on an earlier quest to visit every Lithuanian church in the Chicago area. This one was built in the 1910s by immigrants who barely had money for daily bread but for whom a church with bell towers and domes and stained glass windows was a spiritual and emotional necessity. I understand their priorities; as a girl I used to marvel at the painted ceiling and marble columns of St. Anthony's. The nuns told us we could talk to God anywhere, but, surely, I thought, He listens more intently in a place like this than in some messy bedroom or rat-infested alley.

There was a time when prayer came easily; decades ago, another life. I used to pray that my mother's migraines would stop, that my dad would quit drinking, that my sister would mysteriously disappear. In high school I asked God for a boyfriend who looked like Bob Dylan. I pray now only when I'm flying on airplanes or rushing to buy the last pair of size ten and a half pumps in red before the store closes. Perhaps it is time to try again. I walk in quietly, surprised the church is open on a Friday afternoon.

Toward the front, two young attractive women, one Mexican, one Lithuanian, gaze at each other from opposite walls. Our Lady of Guadalupe, somber in stark blues and orangey yellows, shares holy space with the sweetly smiling figure I've seen in books but can't place. Is she the Mary who appeared to the shepherd children in Šiluva? She's paler in complexion than Aušros Vartų Marija, my favorite virgin version. The face of the original Our Lady of the Gates of Dawn in Vilnius is dark, almost black. The model, historians believe, was Barbora Radvilaitė, the sixteenth-century aristocrat known for her dusky beauty. Every year Lithuanians and Poles by the thousands climb the stairs inside the Gates of Dawn up to the top, some on their knees in supplication, to worship the icon, to marvel at her golden dress, her golden crown, her halo of golden spikes interspersed with tiny golden stars.

This particular representation seems ghostly in comparison, her complexion as pasty as flour.

An important choice awaits me: in front of which Lady to kneel? The two or three other people in the church, older women with tired faces, have put their money on the Guadalupe.

I decide on a pew where I can see both and begin with the first prayer I learned, the Hail Mary in Lithuanian.

Sveika Marija, malonės pilnoji,
Viešpats su Tavimi.

I stop at the next line:

Tu pagirta tarp moterų.

Back in grade school during May devotions Raimundas Mičiulis, whose father owned a tavern, said *girta* instead of *pagirta*, drunk instead of blessed. *You are drunk among women.* Row upon row of second graders stifled titters. The nun, as watchful as a prison guard, understood the magnitude of our misdoing. She seethed—we could sense her seething behind our backs—waiting until the relative privacy of the classroom to administer punishment.

"Prayers said in laughter bounce back and bring disaster," said the nun.

I begin again in English—*Hail Mary, full of grace*—shifting my gaze from one Madonna to the other, back and forth, until they blur into one dizzying vision.

Perhaps the two Marias are not so different after all. Lithuania and Mexico share aspects of a similar Roman Catholicism, one emerging out of the social and economic backgrounds of agrarian life. Lithuania dragged its pagan roots well into the past century; vestiges of the rich Indian culture permeate everyday Mexican life. In both traditions, religious customs predating Christianity fuse with more modern manifestations of Catholic belief, resulting in such practices as the bringing of food to the graves of deceased loved ones on the Feast of All Souls. My Mexican-American students, many with crosses around their necks, write papers on complex Mayan belief systems: "My ancestors were descendents of the gods," one essay begins. A girl I knew would tell me stories of the feathered serpent Kukulcan as if he were a family pet.

By the same token, devout Lithuanian churchgoers boast that Lithuania was the last country in Europe to be baptized. Articles about the pre-Christian past appear regularly not only in scholarly journals but in the mainstream press. In the thirteenth century, when the Magna Carta had been signed in England and Aquinas had published his *Summa contra Gentiles* and international trade was flourishing in Venice, my illiterate ancestors were praying to Perkūnas, the god of Thunder—every Lithuanian schoolchild knows this. They prayed to the sun as well. They worshipped two-trunked trees and kept a holy fire named Gabija burning through the night.

My ancestors believed there were people with special powers; their spells were particularly effective in casting out evil spirits. One way to do this was to guess the name and characteristics of the offending demon and to speculate whether it had lodged in a snake, or in a fire, or in the writhing body of a dying man or woman.

I know your name, the shaman might say. *You are large and gray*; or, *you are brown and striped*, or, *you burn through the night*.

Outside, a light winter rain is falling. The pale afternoon sun has disappeared. I find my way back to Garfield Avenue, which my sister and I would call Garfield Goose Avenue, after our favorite television puppet, the constantly clacking King of the United States on *Garfield Goose and Friends*. I pass the Lithuanian Youth Center on Western Avenue. Now a little island of white ethnicity, surrounded by parking lots and car dealerships and pawn shops, the Center once formed the cornerstone of Lithuanian immigrant social life. The large yellow brick structure is as familiar to me as my childhood home; the stained-glass mosaic that graces the lobby remains a symbol of enchantment—I was always running up to touch the blood-red, deep-purple, and golden-yellow triangles and squares that miraculously formed a picture, of whom I don't remember, St. Casimir, perhaps, or maybe Vytautas the Great?

I make a left on Pulaski, passing the large wooden Indian standing atop the Pearle Vision Center. "How," I whisper and raise my hand, remembering my childhood greeting to the statue. I drive and drive. Pulaski is home to numerous discount tire shops, dentists' offices, and McDonald's. I drive past the Wolniak Funeral Home, Richard J. Daley College, and the Balzekas Museum of Lithuanian Culture. Pulaski—named after the American Revolutionary War hero from Poland. I don't even know whether Pulaski is an avenue or a boulevard or a street. It's always and everywhere just Pulaski.

:.:.:.:.:.:.:.:

She is lying in her bed, a pale blue afghan thrown over her, napping.

My Black Marija.

In the portrait by Petravičius that hangs in the bedroom, my mother's hair is straight and black, her neck long, her nose pronounced. She looks Egyptian. My mother, the Lithuanian Cleopatra.

Marija is her baptismal name. She would have been just Aldona if her grandmother, a God-fearing country woman, hadn't pushed for baptism. Her mother, an educator with socialist politics, had objected, but in this battle of two strong-willed women, my great-grandmother had won out. To this day, my mother's friends from Lithuania call her Maryte, a diminutive of Marija, an endearment. Since stepping off the boat in New York, however, she has gone by her middle name, Aldona.

She wakes up. I help her to the kitchen, where her caretaker, Irutė, is making tea. A bowl of lemons and a plastic container of honey in the shape of a bear stand on the wooden table. Ever since my father died my mother buys only the bear-shaped bottles, with whom she sometimes holds brief conversations—my father's nickname was Big Bear, *Meškis* in Lithuanian.

"Meškis," my mother says, and kisses the plastic bear on its snout.

She never called my father "honey"—*medus* is too sacred a food to ever be a term of endearment. My mother used to serve honey on pieces of cucumber—a special treat.

She'd slice the peeled cucumbers in half, scoop out the seeds, then fill the "boats" with honey.

As a little girl I used to think that honey turned into amber after a few weeks. I'd sneak a cup or two into my room and wait and wait. Once my mother found the honey, as hard as concrete, in my closet. I explained the situation.

"Amber comes from tree resin," she told me. "It takes fifty million years for tree resin to become amber."

I look at my mother and think how slowly things change, yet how often the changes seem external. Tree sap and amber emit the same translucent gold-tinged light. The new immigrant neighborhood is like the old immigrant neighborhood. Religion transforms itself again and again, keeping alive the same underlying need for magic and belief. And my mother's wrinkled face, her balding head contradict the essence of the spirited young woman inside; she can't get up from her chair but stomps her feet when Ellen DeGeneres dances; she loves political jokes—"We Lithuanians have more parties than Hugh Hefner"; she recites snippets from favorite poems, such as Henrikas Radauskas's *The Birth of Song*, with the lucid force of a prophet: "I don't construct buildings, nor lead the nation / I sit beneath the branches of a white acacia tree."

I put my hands around her stomach, hold her from behind while I rub her swollen belly. "I know your name," I say. "You are small and you multiply and you burn through the night."

"What are you doing?" my mother asks.

"Casting out evil spirits."

"Oh," she says, as casually as if I were taking her temperature.

"I prayed for you today, mom. In Lithuanian and in English."

"Good," she smiles. "I need all the help I can get."

A Lithuanian oak

Dreaming Trees

The week before she died, my mother wavered from pain and terror so profound it caused her screams to echo through the hospital corridors at night—to semi-narcosis—to what seemed like relieved, almost comic acceptance.

Three days before my mother's death, my uncle, a noted cancer researcher, kept repeating to the nurses and aides who wouldn't let him see his sister until she was checked into her room, "I am a ducktoor. Ducktoor Valaitis."

"We don't care who you are," one of the aides muttered, and at that moment I felt pity and tenderness for my uncle, a man with whom I'd had my share of differences.

The week before she died, my mother told me to be good to my sister, and to love my husband because he was a good man and worthy of my love.

The week before she died, my mother announced, "I'm going to Brooklyn," and laughed.

Two days before she died, my mother admired the thick dark ringlets of hair on a man "built like an oak." My mother had shared the hospital room with a woman somewhat younger but no less sick than herself. The woman's two sons came to visit.

"Very good-looking," my mother whispered in Lithuanian. "You know which one I mean."

The week before she died, my mother dreamed of trees. She woke up and gazed out the window and saw people trudging across the parking lot to cars that looked like very large coffins.

The week before she died, my mother asked me to recite a poem. Lithuanian poems eluded me like rare birds hidden in the branches of exotic trees. All I could think of was "Oh Country of Heroes" and "The Torches Have Gone Out."

"Can it be in English?" I asked.

She nodded.

I paused, then began, feeling very foolish, "I will arise and go now, and go to Innisfree."

I stumbled on the second line and began to worry that my mother would think I was leaving. But then it all came back to me. The words began to leave my mouth like doves released, one by one, into thick summer air, and when I finished—"I hear it in the deep heart's core"—I had nothing else to say to my mother.

"Beautiful," she said, and closed her eyes, and fell asleep.

The day before she died my mother asked for last rites. The priest rubbed some balm on her forehead with his thumb and sprinkled her with water. He held her hand for a very long time. We prayed the Our Father, my sister, the priest, and I—*Tėve Mūsų, Kuris esi danguje*—and when we got to the end my mother whispered *amen*, her last two syllables on this weary earth.

In the corridor I handed the priest fifty dollars.

"I can't take money for this," he said.

He'd been in this country for only a few years; he looked tired and sad. He had held my mother's hand for such a very long time.

"Please," I said. "It will make me feel better."

My great-grandmother's grave in Lithuania

The Lithuanian Book of the Dead

When my grandmother died, at eighty-six, her mind had lost its former suppleness. She had lived across the alley from us in Cicero and sometimes wandered the neighborhood, ending up once or twice knocking on the door of the Stakulis's asking to speak to my mother or, if my mother wasn't there, to listen to their transistor radio.

My mother refused to send her to a nursing home until the very end, when it was clear that she needed more than daily visits from the family and an occasional helpful neighbor. She spent her last days at the Holy Family Villa, a nursing home not far from the hospital where my uncle worked as head pathologist. We had come to see her only a few times as a family, which makes me think she couldn't have been there long. My mother was made distraught by these visits, not so much by the sight of my grandmother, sitting there limply, her heavy legs covered by a pale blue afghan, smiling to have such distinguished visitors, but by a man who kept mistaking my mother for a rabbit.

Before her death, my grandmother appeared to my mother in a vision, riding in on a wave of warmth and color. The intensity of the encounter brought my mother to tears. She was in the hospital herself, suffering either a common female malady or a minor nervous breakdown. My mother's explanations of the cause changed over time, varying with audience and mood. Minutes after the apparition a nurse announced that the doctor had just called from Holy Family; my grandmother had died.

During my mother's final weeks—an inevitable end the doctors timed almost to the day—I had hoped for a similar revelation. I imagined her soul escaping the confines of her withered body, flittering above me as I drank my morning coffee, waving good-bye, good luck, a few strains of Debussy's *La Mer* as background music. There had been no appearance, of course, though when I called Irute, my mother's caretaker and constant companion during these last few difficult months, she said the washing machine had stopped working and that the refrigerator light, not overly bright to begin with, had dimmed considerably.

"To be expected, of course," she said in Lithuanian.

Centuries ago in Lithuania the unearthly moaning of an owl signified that a nearby soul had left its body and was searching for a new home—a tree or wild animal in which to abide. Today the Lithuanian herald of death seems to be the breakdown of common household appliances.

Marty and I are sitting in the spacious modern office of the Petkus Funeral Home in Tinley Park, paging through a large leather-bound book of casket designs. A computer whirs gently in the background. A gilded photograph of the Chicago White Sox hangs on the wall.

"You can always go with the model your mom chose for your dad," the undertaker, whom I'll call Vince, suggests.

I don't remember the casket, nor do I remember this middle-aged man having been in charge of funeral arrangements made more than fifteen years ago. Although in many ways he is no different from many

Lithuanian men—he carries his extra weight around his stomach, his ruddy complexion suggests a propensity for beer—there is something else familiar about him, something that suggests a previous connection, perhaps on the rough-and-tumble streets of Cicero.

"That would be appropriate," I say, relieved to have to make one fewer decision.

Vince asks what I've chosen for my mother's burial garment. I show him the teal-blue silk dress she wore for special occasions.

"Nice."

"And these amber beads. She liked these."

"What about underwear?"

"What *about* underwear?"

"It was one of Mr. Petkus's firmest beliefs that no person should ever be buried without clean underwear."

You've got to be kidding, I want to say, but I don't want to come off as disrespectful, the kind of Lithuanian daughter who cannot properly bury her mother.

"I guess I'll have to go back for, uh, panties and bra."

"Is there anything your mother would want to take with her to the grave?" he asks.

"What do you mean?"

"Last year a woman insisted her husband be buried with a bottle of his favorite vodka."

"My mother wasn't a drinker."

"And some guy had written in his will that a dozen bacon buns from Baltic Bakery be placed in the casket."

"No, no bacon buns."

"Manicure?" he asks.

For a moment I imagine he is urging me to get my nails done and is offering to do the job himself.

"Your mother's nails," he says.

"Uh, okay. Just file them down a bit. And maybe some pink polish, nothing too bright."

"Rosary?"

"No, my mother wasn't really a rosary kind of person."

"*Capisce*. It's just that holding a rosary makes it look like your mother's doing something."

"As opposed to?"

"As opposed to twiddling her thumbs."

"No. No rosary."

He assures me that my mother will look fine, that he does the "work" himself.

As we continue talking I realize, with a slowly growing sense of horror, that years ago I had gotten drunk with this man at one of the bars on Sixty-Ninth Street or maybe at some South Side party. More than that, I had known him, or had almost known him, in the biblical sense, had drunk of the liquor of his generous kisses, had run my fingers through his now-thinning blond hair. It's clear by the pleasant, professional expression on his face that he doesn't remember—or has preferred to forget—the whole sordid adventure.

As he walks us to the door, Vince talks about the old neighborhood, about the three funeral homes on one residential block—Fiftieth Avenue—with Petkus only a half block down from Vance.

"Death Row," he says. "That's what we used to call it."

How convenient this must have been in the 1920s and 1930s when people were always dying, of tuberculosis and emphysema and syphilis and cirrhosis of the liver, young women in childbirth, and infants from whooping cough and unpasteurized milk. I remember reading in a history of Chicago how Lithuanian women in Bridgeport would walk from parlor to parlor—they didn't have to know the dead to be welcome—and collect holy cards of the saints and catch up on neighborhood gossip.

"Death Row," I nod.

I think of all of the Lithuanian wakes I've been to as a child. I remember the sensation of coldness; outside the August heat might be rippling in waves, or the hesitant warmth of late April lingering in the air, but inside the funeral home a perpetual winter existed, a world of stillness and chill. My progressive parents had gone to great lengths to explain the naturalness of death, yet everything had seemed artificial, the pale lilac draperies, as stiff as an Elizabethan muff, the rigid white shirred satin of the coffin lining, the face of the corpse like week-old Wonder bread.

It is not my mother's body laid out like an artifact in her special teal-blue dress that makes me want to cry, rather it is the people entering the room—slowly, because this is not a place where one rushes, but also because they are old. They trickle in at first—those who have the afternoon to spare and for whom a wake provides the chance not only to pay respects but also to discuss the recent political debacles in Lithuania and the latest accomplishments of their brilliant grandchildren. As the afternoon wears on, more come piling in, childhood friends who knew my mother as Marytė, women from the neighborhood with whom she drank tea and occasionally bickered, her aging Lithuanian Girl Scout troop. They bring a peace lily in a wicker basket, a welcome change from the monumental wreaths of scarlet roses and stifling white carnations.

Some of the visitors have brought cameras, not because my mother was a celebrity, but because this is what Lithuanians do—they line up in front of the casket, sometimes in groups of twos or threes, and take pictures of themselves with the recently deceased. Somewhere in my mother's basement there are pictures of the entire family posed in front of my grandmother's casket as rigid as marionettes, looking grimly into the camera, except for my grandfather, who stares directly at my grandmother's face, his heart breaking. A friend of my mother's even keeps a scrapbook of wakes she has been to—page after page of photos reveal a woman growing older in front of our very eyes, yet wearing the same bouffant hairdo, standing stiffly in front of friends and relatives not as fortunate as she.

By seven the funeral home is packed. Arvid appears, late, as usual.

"I like your priest outfit," I tell him.

I await a typical response, "I like your madwoman costume," but he hugs me instead, holds me close like the good friend he is.

We go over the details of the service, who will speak first, what prayers will be said. My fear is that Arvid will monopolize the time with yet another episode of the *Father Arvid Show*, that he will recreate the neighborhood of our youth, painting detailed portraits of what it was like living next to the Markelis family before finally getting to the virtues of my mother. But his eulogy is fairly short, at least in Arvid Time.

He talks about my mother's kindness, her sense of humor, her creativity.

He tells the story of when he was twelve and his parents bought him a red winter coat. Kids made fun of the coat, which was bought on clearance. "Nobody has a red coat, Arvid," they laughed.

He sought my mother's advice.

"You are not the kind of boy to wear a gray or a black coat, Arvid," she counseled. "You are an original. And you have a beautiful red coat."

The morning of the funeral it is drizzling. The heavy bloated clouds threaten harder rain.

"If you want to know what I think," says my sister in the hearse.

No one says anything.

"I think ma knows that we're all feeling sad," she continues. "That's why it's raining."

Dead only three days, and already my mother is in charge of the weather.

Remnants of belief linger like the fleeting images of recurring dreams. I often dream that I am lost; lost on the Eisenhower Expressway, or lost at the International Lithuanian Folk Dance Festival at the Chicago Amphitheater, or lost in the forests of Camp Rakas. In some of these dreams I find my way home through unmarked wooden paths or hidden signs suddenly revealing themselves as exits. In others I search for landmarks and familiar street names as the sun begins to set. I begin to run, faster and faster as darkness engulfs the remaining vestiges of graying light. I wake up crying. The day after these nightmares I move slowly, carefully, scrutinizing the world for omens. I double-check the locks. I listen to weather reports for tornado warnings, possible blizzards.

The early Lithuanians believed that dreams foretold the future. If you dream you've lost a tooth, someone will die soon. If your parents call your name, *you* will die soon. They believed that snakes brought good luck; they kept bowls of milk for their household serpents. They believed that after death women turned into ducks or cuckoos, men into ravens or roosters. Or they changed into trees—lindens and oaks and birches and spruce. The early Lithuanians believed that the dead must be buried away from home, preferably on a treeless hilltop, lest a careless son or vengeful neighbor chop down a family member / tree.

Despite years of Catholic schooling, it is easier to see my mother's soul searching for its childhood home than living in a quiet, proper Christian heaven. But the house in Marijampolė is no longer there, replaced by a concrete apartment complex built under the Soviets. My mother's soul flees to the shores of the Baltic Sea in Klaipėda where as a girl she had gathered amber in the mornings following a storm. But the water is polluted. *Russian industry*, claims my mother's soul, and flies back west to Charleston, Illinois, to the giant oak tree in the backyard of our house.

This coming autumn acorns will skitter across our roof like tiny feet, and I will hear my mother's voice. In December the morning snow will settle on the branches of the oak, shifting lightly with the slightest wind. I will see my mother in the brittle shadows of winter birds.

Acknowledgments

First and foremost, I'd like to thank the EIU Writer Babes: Ruth Hoberman, Mary Maddox, Letitia Moffitt, and Angela Vietto. You've been there from the beginning—your insightful suggestions, unwavering support, and really good snacks have made this memoir possible. Thanks as well to those who've commented on earlier drafts of chapters: John Kilgore, Miho Nonaka, Francine McGregor, Jad Smith, and the late Marty Scott. *Širdingas ačiu* to Violeta Kelertas: critic, writer, mentor, role model.

Robert P. Devens: you are extraordinary, and not only because you accepted my manuscript. If there were a Lithuanian God of Editors, you would be he. Anne Summers Goldberg, you're pretty special yourself. Your patience, professionalism, and good humor have made this process enjoyable. Thanks to Mark Reschke, for making this a more readable manuscript. I'm grateful for the constructive criticism provided by the two readers chosen by the press: Achy Obejas and Benjamin Paloff.

I am indebted to Eastern Illinois University, which made it possible for me to work on this book through a summer research and creative activity grant, a sabbatical, and a course release. And thank you, Dana Ringuette, for giving me the chance to change my colors.

I'd also like to thank Dagni Bredesen, Jeanne Herrick, Debra Arment Valentino, Terese Boguta, and Daina Pakalnis for their suggestions, friendship, and support; Elena Namikas and Andrius Drevinskas for their photographs; and Father Arvydas Žygas for just being who he is.

Finally, to my husband, Marty Gabriel, life partner, best friend, and honorary Lithuanian—the next book is about you.